WHY DID TRUMP WIN?

CHRONICLING THE STAGES OF NEOLIBERAL REACTIONISM DURING AMERICA'S MOST TURBULENT ELECTION CYCLE

ANIS SHIVANI

FUturist Press
Houston, Boston, Los Angeles

Copyright © 2017 by FUturist Press: A Coalition for Millennial Change

All rights reserved. No part of this book may be reproduced, in any form, without written permission from the publisher.

Requests for permission to reproduce selections from this book should be directed to: Permissions Department, FUturist Press, 2041 Norfolk Street, Houston, Texas 77098, or FUturist.Press@gmail.com.

Published in the United States by FUturist Press, Houston, Texas 77098

LIBRARY OF CONGRESS CATALOGING-IN-PUBLICATION DATA

Why Did Trump Win: Chronicling the Stages of Neoliberal Reactionism During America's Most Turbulent Election Cycle / Anis Shivani
ISBN: 978-1542665056
1. Neofascism—Cultural Aspects—United States. 2. Donald J. Trump—Cultural Appeal—United States. 3. Neoliberalism—Political Conditions—2001-. 4. United States—Political Conditions—2001-.

FUturist Press was established in 2017 as an unorthodox alternative to the neoliberal aesthetic currently dominating the book publishing industry. FUturist Press operates in the public interest and is committed to publishing, in innovative ways taking advantage of current technologies, works of significant cultural, aesthetic, philosophical, and moral value that are often deemed not marketable enough by both large and small publishers.

www.thefuturistpress.com

Composition by FU-fu!
This book was set in Garamond Pro

Printed in the United States of America

2 4 6 8 9 7 5 3 1

FUturist Press: A Coalition for Millennial Change publishes fine books of elegantly-written polemics, aesthetic statements, philosophical investigations, moral and cultural criticism, and imaginative writing driven by eclectic, personal, idiosyncratic knowledge of the humanist disciplines; we seek to change the discourse around politics, literature, and art by discovering ideas that have yet to take shape, not regurgitate the ones already known and understood. Stay tuned for our future offerings!

By the Same Author

Anatolia and Other Stories
The Fifth Lash and Other Stories

Karachi Raj: A Novel
A History of the Cat in Nine Chapters or Less

My Tranquil War and Other Poems
Whatever Speaks on Behalf of Hashish: Poems
Soraya: Sonnets
The Moon Blooms in Occupied Hours: Poems
Confessions I: Poems

Against the Workshop: Provocations, Polemics, Controversies
Literary Writing in the Twenty-First Century: Conversations

V

While the aristocratic man lives confidently and is open to himself (γεννηθεί, "noble-born," emphasizes the nuance "sincere," and perhaps also "naïve"), the man of resentment, on the other hand, is not sincere or naïve, neither honest nor candid with himself. His soul *squints*; his mind loves dark corners, secret passages and hidden doors, everything covert appeals to him as *his* world, *his* security, *his* comfort; he is a past master of silence, of not forgetting, of patience, of assuming a mode of self-deprecation and humility for a while. A race of such *resentful* men will eventually prove *more cunning* than any aristocratic race; they will respect cunning to a much greater degree, namely as something most vital to existence, whereas cunning among aristocratic men is apt to be redolent of luxury and refinement; so among them it does not play so integral a part as that complete certainty of function of the governing unconscious instincts, nor as that certain lack of caution, such as a valiant charge at the enemy, bravery in the face of danger, or as those ecstatic bursts of rage, love, reverence, gratitude, by which at all times noble souls have recognized each other. When the resentment of the aristocratic man manifests itself, it is consumed and exhausted in an immediate reaction, and consequently instills no venom; on the other hand, it never manifests itself at all in countless instances when it would be inevitable for the feeble and weak.

— Friedrich Nietzsche, *On the Genealogy of Morals*

To all those clear-minded enough to separate the truth from lies

Contents

Acknowledgments / x

Preface / xi

1. Fascist Trump, Neoliberal Hillary, Progressive Bernie: Three Contrasting Rhetorical Styles / 1

2. Where Does Sanders Go from Here: Strategy, Vision, and Eloquence in the Rise of the New Progressivism / 9

3. The Brooklyn Debate: Bernie Sanders Has Altered the Terms of Discourse / 13

4. The Unraveling of the Two-Party System and the Desperation of the Elites / 18

5. Five-Alarm Panic in Progress: Should We Listen to the Hypocritical Elites Who Can't Even Own up to Trump? / 24

6. What, Exactly, Is Neoliberalism: And Why Should We Care Beyond the Current Election Campaign / 29

7. Feminists, Stop Obfuscating: Hillary Clinton Does *Not* Represent Values That Help Women / 42

8. Hillarybots, You Blew It! Thanks for Another Decade of War, Misery, and Scandal / 48

9. Donald Trump Is Going to Win: This Is Why Hillary Clinton Can Never Defeat What Trump Represents / 53

10. The Millennial Generation Is a Perfect Fit for Socialism / 60

11. Thank You, Donald Trump: The Left Ignores the Intellectual Substance of Trumpism at Its Own Peril / 64

12. Why Did Donald Trump Win? / 78

13. Forty Short Post-Election Theses: Where Do We Stand Now and Where Do We Go from Here / 83

14. The Coming Immigration Crisis: The First Battle of the Trump Administration / 90

15. Quit America: The Case for Moral Disengagement from American Politics / 96

16. Is Trump Cut from the Same Cloth as Mussolini? Eleven Key Lessons from Historical Fascism / 109

About the Author / 123

Acknowledgments

The essays in this volume appeared in *AlterNet*, *Counterpunch*, *Huffington Post*, *Salon*, *State of Nature: An Online Journal of Radical Ideas*, *Truthdig*, *Truthout*, and *OpEd News*. My deep gratitude in particular to Cihan Aksan, Dave Daley, Don Hazen, Andrew O'Hehir, Rob Kall, Jeffrey St. Clair, and Britney Schultz for publishing them. My thanks also to the individual writers at many different blogs such as Naked Capitalism, Liberty Blitzkrieg, Washington Spectator, the Spinoff, PJ Media, Futures Magazine, The Wild Reed, The Vanishing Mediator, Booman Tribune, Outside the Beltway, Newsweek.com, The Modurban Liberal, Public Skeleton, CartaCapital, Coldwater Economics, Authentically Wired, Brecha, Progressive Radio Network, 3QuarksDaily, and many others besides, who took the time to circulate and discuss these essays during the course of the election campaign. Many thanks to Michael Woodson at Pacifica radio in Houston for frequently hosting me to air out these views, and also to Garland Nixon at Pacifica radio in Washington, DC for providing a platform to discuss these ideas. Thanks to Dylan Bergeson at Al-Jazeera Plus for hosting a post-election discussion. Thank you, all!

Cover Art: *Evening Dress (Habit de Rigueur)* By Alexandra Exter 1926, wood, cardboard, plastic, and material, 33 x 13 1/2 x 8 in. Courtesy Los Angeles County Museum of Art

Preface

At the beginning of 2017, we are in unprecedented territory. A man with overtly fascist leanings, someone right out of a dystopian movie script or science fiction novel, has stepped up to take charge of all of our destinies. Activists feel helpless, thinkers and planners outwitted, humanitarians overwhelmed, politicians irrelevant, and the ordinary citizen with a low level of political engagement tries not to think too hard about how this came about and what it means for our future. All we know for certain is that things are going to change, very soon, and very hard—and then what happens is anyone's guess. Will the institutions provide checks against authoritarian power? Will there be a return to humanist values, despite all odds? Will compassion and mercy and empathy toward marginalized groups make a comeback, even though the social darwinists have won the day for now?

The polity hangs in the balance, though it was not supposed to be this way, if you ask the establishment thinkers and politicians. By now a second chapter in what is propagated as the ongoing multicultural success of twenty-first-century America was about to be inaugurated, with the policies of the last quarter-century reaching their next stage of culmination. But was it really as rosy a picture as those who would have liked continuity recall in their current moment of angst? Had there not been immeasurable anxiety, insecurity, and dissatisfaction—resentment, yes—among large swaths of the population, the future that we are facing now, with the militaristic, xenophobic, nativist, protectionist, antiglobalist, antiliberal, antiscientific options on the table, would not have come about. From the beginning, I thought Trump was all but inevitable, and explained why I thought this was so, and why Hillary was the most compromised and unelectable modern American candidate I had seen. I also explained, at different points in the campaign, Bernie Sanders's appeal to our better natures, how he seemed to me a last shot at redemption, after President Obama had failed to provide any semblance of accountability and truth-seeking with regard to the sins and the crimes of the preceding eight years. Sanders's loss was a heartbreak, because history took a sharp turn toward a brutal, violent, unpredictable direction at that point.

As these essays were written in response to the flux and turmoil of the brutally divisive—but utterly clarifying—election, they consistently take on the institutional causes for the change in direction that has just taken place. In charting the philosophical contours of this election campaign as seen from left, right, and center, I am not interested in personalities per se, but only as they reflect underlying economic or material realities. It was possible for me to foresee what was going to happen, as you will note about these essays again and again, but not because I am possessed of some magic foresight or rare powers of prophecy. Anyone clear-eyed about our "neoliberal nightmare"—as one *Salon* headline had it above one of my central articles in this book—would have been able to perceive where things were going. Being taken by surprise by Trump also means that a citizen is so caught up in one's own position in the social spectrum that anything outside it is unreachable, therefore unable to enter into one's planning and calculation. That is not a good outcome for democracy; such division and separation can only have tragic consequences. I hope what's different about this book is my level of sympathy for positions that are alien to my own inclination. It is not that difficult to see things from the point of view of the other side; in fact it's rather difficult *not* to see things from the point of view of the other side, it takes quite a bit of doing.

The essays in this book respond to this fear of the other, this inability to comprehend empirical reality, when it interferes with the continuation of the social status each of us has already attained. In a way, each of these essays was a rupture with the image of continuity—thus causing a lot of reaction in the blogosphere and discussion forums—amongst citizens who were caught up in the spectacle of the thing, the explicit overtones of apocalypse that were raining down upon us instead of our usual quota of political news. When I predicted in May that Trump would win, the entire right-wing ecosphere went crazy—Breitbart, RedState, Limbaugh, Drudge, and the rest—because an obviously progressive, anarchistically inclined socialist liberal was breaking from the lip service journalists on the left were supposed to pay to the moral goodness of "our side" while demonizing and brutalizing the "other side." But I say, in these essays, that both sides are being played; there is no "our side" or "their side," there is only an out-of-control capitalism in final confrontation with the planet and all living beings, and all of us, on all sides, are the ultimate victims.

I hope this book provides some thought-provoking ideas, no matter the nature of your political commitment, about the state of American politics—which really means our own state as citizens, how we balance different desires and values that play into democratic coherence, and how we read (and perhaps heal) the fissures and overlaps that are redefining American democracy at a truly rapid pace.

Anis Shivani
Houston, Texas
June 1, 2017

Fascist Trump, Neoliberal Hillary, and Progressive Bernie: Three Contrasting Rhetorical Styles

I was curious about the big show of humanity Donald Trump assembled in the old Dixie stronghold of Mobile, Alabama, supported by nativist Senator Jeff Sessions, so I watched the entire Trump Alabama rally,[1] and some others of his too. Trump was surprisingly entertaining, for the limited range of ideas he possesses, and at this point I find it hard to pull away from any of his antics.

At first glance Trump would seem to fit the mold of the pure fascist better than George W. Bush, but in the end I would have to conclude that this is not quite the case. I'm always cautious about applying the term fascist, though I did so to the project I saw emerging (though never fully realized) during the peak of belligerence in the early Bush years,[2] and I also reevaluated my early judgment and brought the situation up to date in the aftermath of the 2012 election.[3]

Trump's entire spiel is centered around how *they*—the immigrants, foreign countries like China and Mexico—have screwed us out of the wealth and prosperity we deserve, and how he, the duly elected strongman (though he wishes there were no elections and he could get in to do the job of the "killer" negotiator based on the strength of current polls alone) will outwit and outmuscle these wily powers (it's always the state he rails against, or corporations and entities backed by the state) to regain America's fair share; just as he personally embodies the American state, he will take on diverse states personified by other individuals like "Abi" of Japan. Oh, he loves the Saudis, the Chinese, even the Mexicans, how could he not, they buy his properties for forty million dollars, they

---
[1] https://www.youtube.com/watch?v=zrBx3eRnKDE.
[2] See, for instance, my essay, "Is America Becoming Fascist?," published in 2002: http://www.counterpunch.org/2002/10/26/is-america-becoming-fascist/.
[3] My reassessment, ten years after first discussing fascism in America, is here: http://www.stateofnature.org/?p=7192.

have money and he must do business with them, but he will execute the "art of the deal," which he knows better than any diplomatic namby-pamby like Caroline Kennedy or any other political appointee, and thereby *make America great again*.

America has been made weak by those without patriotic feeling, politicians who sell the country down the drain on behalf of corporations like Ford and Nabisco which relocate abroad. The only thing that will save us is when America becomes profitable again, but profits must be procured in the name of the nation, and he, Trump, will hire the kind of "horrible" people who will ensure such profits on our behalf.

Trump is a continuous stream-of-consciousness articulator of all the ignorant resentments—against uppity women and gays and African Americans and Hispanics and Asians, against Germany and Japan and Korea whom we still "protect" at great cost without getting anything in return, against Middle Eastern countries whom we strengthen and support at the cost of our only ally Israel—that I first heard injected in the body politic about twenty-five years ago when right-wing talk radio came into its own.

Trump's spiel is a compilation of every uninformed, simplistic, and delusional component of the conspiratorial narrative of grievance held by "real" Americans against those who are said to have falsely appropriated the label "American" for themselves.[1] Trump, like all the ignorant demagogues preceding him, claims that he will clean up this mess and separate the true Americans from the

But does all this add up to fascism?

Fascism is the alliance of big business with the military in a nationalist rejuvenation that aims to regain lost greatness by resorting to violence and brutality. Trump does say he's the "most militaristic" guy you will know, and echoes Bush from the 2000 campaign and all subsequent Republican frontrunners that he will "rebuild" the military. He wants the military to be so strong that we will never have to use it. His attitude toward corporations is that they need to be brought in line with the country's needs, they need to act patriotic rather than greedy by keeping jobs in America, otherwise he will tax them disproportionately if they build or send jobs overseas. He's not about to start any wars—or at least he hasn't said so yet—to bring back the luster to our glory. He does

lxxviiilxxviiilxxviii—————————————
[1] Trump outlines his nationalist views to Oprah Winfrey in 1988: https://www.youtube.com/watch?v=SEPs17_AkTI.

introduce the element of charisma, something I always noted was missing during the Bush years, because, entertainer that he is, he knows how to speak to the people in just the right folksy manner that reiterates their every prejudice while simultaneously holding himself apart (because of his wealth) as a super-special specimen of humanity.

I leave it as an open question the degree to which this act is genuine and heartfelt or simply a way to tap into the narrative of resentment and accompanying aspiration for national regeneration that is ever the story of fascist insurgency. It's not really a relevant question anyway, as long as we recognize the style.

For Trump, as for all his fascist predecessors, it is *democracy itself* which gets in the way of achieving greatness, performing those heroic deeds, for which the tired, weakened, aggrieved nation of true patriots yearns. It is democracy itself which must be circumvented and sidelined. Except in the case of Trump, it is not Middle Eastern domination or the end to terror worldwide that he's after, but simply negotiating better deals with China and Mexico.

Fascist leaders have a way of appearing like clowns to rational liberal observers. This was true of Mussolini, Hitler, and lately Bush. It is hard to believe that with their ludicrous explanations of the way the world works they can gain any traction, but they always become enormously popular in the blink of an eye and the rationalist intelligentsia rub their eyes in disbelief. Precisely the same thing is happening with Trump now.

Consider the originator of fascism, Mussolini, and notice the remarkable similarities between his and Trump's performances: the same supercilious mockery of democrats, journalists, liberals, human rights campaigners, do-gooders; the same puerile postures and gestures, hard to imagine on a national stage except that it is actually happening; the same denial of past history and present circumstances in favor of creating a brand-new reality in accordance with the wishes of the adoring masses; the same preening self-admiration as the hero who alone embodies the wishes of the outwitted, outmaneuvered, outgunned people and will lead them to salvation; the same identification of nation with leader, until Mussolini (or Trump) becomes the nation, until the nation is unimaginable without him as its singular reincarnation.[1]

lxxviiilxxviiilxxviii————————————————
[1] Here is one of Mussolini's classic performances: https://www.youtube.com/watch?v=rn81ysnsBzU.

The war drums and patriotic music are missing, for now, and it is all done with a self-referential, ironic, calculated cool—the subtext of Trump's performance is always that it is a performance after all, as is all politics, so we better get used to his perpetual mockery of the performance at the meta-level—that goes down well with consumers of reality TV.

What led to all this, to Trump's emergence, to this new insanity?

I would like to go back to Hillary Clinton's embodiment of the corrupt liberal style fascists like Trump are always assailing, beginning with her contentless book tour of last summer (2014) and punctuated by her opening campaign commercial, a terrifying advertisement for a neoliberal fantasy seeking to dismiss economic reality, as completely out of tune with present circumstances as Trump's fascist fantasy. Hillary's campaign commercial bothered me no end when it came out in April (2015), and it hasn't let go of me yet.[1] It begs to be deconstructed frame by frame for the delusional economic exceptionalism it propounds. It's a vision of a neoliberal America based on an imagined meritocracy that is as frightening as it is vacuous and severe and unforgiving. One mistake, in this world of strict rules and upward mobility, and you're done.

Here are the folks, the real *everyday Americans*—in her own liberal way, Hillary wants to continue the necessary segregation between real and fake Americans as assiduously as Trump—Hillary wants to give a chance at a better school, a bigger home, an entrepreneurial venture, a path forward in the professional world. Except that Hillary is not actually going to do a single thing for them; as she has explained in subsequent campaign speeches, these are the (righteous) folks who "fought their way back" on their own and pulled themselves up by the bootstraps during the economic crisis (the one during which Hillary was senator). It's just—their time—you know. They're not the ones who needed to be bailed out from unsustainable mortgage or student loan debt—Bernie's people—they are the ones who *made it*. Every one of the people in her commercial smacks of liberal virtue, having paid their dues and followed every little rule on the path to success. Well, regardless of who gets elected, it's these people's time anyway, the righteous professionals already run the show.

Yes, I'm blaming it all on Hillary—or rather, the establishment neoliberal capitalists who've selected her as their figurehead/messenger

---
[1] Hillary Clinton's opening campaign commercial:
https://www.youtube.com/watch?v=N708P-A45D0.

this time around (Jeb would serve just fine too, only at the margins is he any different than Hillary, so a Hillary-Jeb contest leaves them winners in every way). Fascism, or any form of political reaction, occurs only when liberals leave the field empty. And Hillary is leaving it emptier, blanker, seedier, more nondescript than any candidate I've seen in the Democratic party since the neoliberal ascendancy, more even than Al Gore, John Kerry, or Barack Obama. In that sense, she is the worst modern candidate ever.

And she never learns. Compare her rallies in New York and Iowa after Bernie Sanders had climbed in the polls with later rallies and you'll see no difference.[1] It's the same basic script, the same faux populism that neoliberals have been using since the 2000 Gore campaign, doctored by maestros such as Bob Shrum, using the same blank rhetoric about "fighting" for the middle-class and wanting to be the president of "all" Americans, not just "the few." She even wants to work across the aisle to keep us "safe" from terror, that's one of her four fights; and there's even "reinventing government," recycled from Al Gore's failed venture.

I wonder at the chutzpah of this politician whose husband's administration accelerated the apocalyptic decline of the working class and the middle class, particularly after the 1994 electoral debacle. She who, along with her husband, jettisoned core Democratic principles such as single-payer health care, gave in to right-wing discourse on every single social policy, and gutted the New Deal and Great Society consensus on education, taxes, budgets, welfare, immigration, telecommunications, crime, banking, and trade, now wants to "fight" on behalf of the very people whose decimation is associated with Clintonism even more than with Reaganism.[2] And she offers not a single policy prescription of substance, besides platitudes about rewarding hard work and playing by the rules (just as her husband did), as you can see from her rallies and speeches. Had she not left such a complete vacuum of policy and failed to address the real economic misery out there, there would have been no opening for Trump or other extremists.

lxxviiilxxviiilxxviii——————————————

[1] Clinton's opening campaign rally in June 2015:
https://www.youtube.com/watch?v=bNpIWB5MT78.
[2] Clinton unequivocally rejecting gay marriage in 2004:
https://www.youtube.com/watch?v=yRzQKXguZVI. Equal rights for LGBTQ people is suddenly, along with support for "hardworking" and "taxpaying" immigrants, one of the subsets of her "four fights."

Bernie Sanders, on the other hand, offers specific policies—not just rhetoric—on each and every economic and social crisis that Hillary mentions and then sidelines in fuzzy words. Before Clintonism demolished core Democratic principles, as in the endorsement of managed care (i.e., privatized health care) rather than the single-payer Medicare-type health care Bernie advocates, all of Bernie's prescriptions used to be mainstream liberal aspirations. I hope he jettisons his self-declared label of "democratic socialist"—he's hardly a democratic socialist in the European vein, but rather a pretty conventional New Deal progressive, and actually harkens back even farther to the beginnings of the Progressive movement. He wants free higher education (which more or less used to be the case anyway for most students before rapid tuition inflation put paid to that in the last generation or so), a $15 minimum wage (already that figure is becoming outdated), and Medicare for all—hardly "socialist" prescriptions.[1]

Bernie is the scholar-gentleman—a Ralph Nader with charisma—that this country desperately needs. Consider his measured, tolerant, patient response to Black Lives Matter disrupters at two events, in Seattle[2] and the Netroots gathering,[3] to the fascist bluster of Trump in kicking out anchor Jorge Ramos of Univision[4] (for Bernie, it is always about what the people need, in terms of specific policies that have zero echo in Hillary's world, while for Trump it is always about himself, bragging for instance about his $500 million lawsuit against Univision even as he throws quite the whiny fascist tantrum at the press conference):

And isn't it ironic that the Black Lives Matter protestors would be interested in going above all after Bernie, the one candidate who actually has their interest at heart, proposing real criminal justice reform and economic rehabilitation on a mass scale, compared to all the other fakes running for president? Black Lives Matter activists note correctly that it was neoliberal repression in the 1990s that set the stage for the current wave of mass incarceration and police brutality.

---

[1] Bernie Sanders rally in Wisconsin, Madison, early in the campaign: https://www.youtube.com/watch?v=OewBDIwy-O4.
[2] Sanders calmly handles Black Lives Matter protestors who disrupted his early Seattle rally: https://www.youtube.com/watch?v=oV-ZSP0zAuI.
[3] Sanders again showing great empathy in dealing with BLM protestors at the Netroots convention: https://www.youtube.com/watch?v=ElcJy5yZfvk.
[4] Trump kicks out Univision anchor Jorge Ramos from an early rally: https://www.youtube.com/watch?v=pbIT7Jfj9jw.

So there we have it, the style we need and deserve (Bernie's, offering not just hollow words that have had all the meaning rubbed out of them after a generation of Clinton-Bush-Obama neoliberalism, but real solutions for real problems),[1] versus Trump's inverted populism, or fascism if you like to use that language (imagine every sane proposal offered by Bernie turned on its head, so that it becomes a privatized, ruthless, brutal policy benefiting the rich even more than they already do, because after all we can all aspire to become rich like Trump), and the scariest of all, Hillary. No, it is not Trump who scares me—Trump at least lays it out in the open, let's have Trump and Sanders be the nominees and go at it with all they've got, representing the Republican and Democratic bases at their core—but Hillary, with her delusional meritocracy in a world that's become geared to benefiting only the already advantaged.

Contrast Bernie's speeches—and his policy platform online—point by point with Hillary's, and you'll see each and every concrete proposal, rooted in economic sanity, meet with an illusory and fake one, such as "making college affordable." Yes, Hillary, how? Why can't you just say that public education will be free, as it pretty much used to be before inflation and privatization and deregulation distorted the social bargain in the 1990s?

Hillary is making Bill Clinton look really bad. There was an afterglow about some aspects of the Clinton presidency—at least he made globalization at the rhetorical level acceptable, rather than the inwardness of the cold war years, and even if said globalization was deeply flawed at the structural level, by the time Seattle 1999 rolled around there was at least the promise that its flaws could be addressed in the emergence of a global cosmopolitan order based on rights and duties—but Hillary has ruined what remained of the image, pulling out the same bag of nonsensical micro-initiatives that doomed the opportunities provided by the peace that followed the end of the cold war. She can't change because it is all she and the people she represents, the neoliberal ruling class, have to offer. We can expect nothing beyond that from her, except more intensified paeans to American exceptionalism.

While I regret the element of economic nationalism that has crept into progressive thinking and feel sorry about the loss of faith in trade and openness in favor of a hunkered-down protectionism, this is something

---
[1] Read Bernie Sanders's policy platform online: https://berniesanders.com/issues/.

that infects the entire left, and is a legacy of the flawed inception of globalization in the Clinton years. The only way around that—to find our way back, really—is to make ours a more humane society, with exactly the kind of redistribution downward that Bernie is talking about, so that a freer, more open, more trusting world can once again emerge on the horizon. In that sense, I have total empathy with Bernie and his rhetoric. And then there's the perverted economic nationalism of Trump, rooted in white supremacy and a xenophobic victimization that has no basis in reality given our unparalleled national wealth and resources.

In pre-fascist Italy, at least, the gains in terms of expanding democracy and prosperity were real; it was a revolution of rising expectations, as Tocqueville would have it, that led to the fascist upsurge in the teens and twenties of the twentieth century not only in Italy but elsewhere as well. But the Clintons hollowed out the American economy and as a consequence the social bargain, introducing the absolute dominance of corporations that immiserated Americans; even as she spouts mindless rhetoric, Hillary wants to extend precisely that project forward.

Where Does Bernie Sanders Go from Here? Strategy, Vision, and Eloquence in the Rise of the New Progressivism

If anyone was ever less in need of strategic advice than Bernie Sanders at this point in his campaign, I don't know who that would be. In that sense my thoughts are redundant, but it seems helpful to put them down anyway for the sake of clarity as we move into the next phase of this campaign.

Already Sanders is showing swift-footedness in making all the moves necessary to not only establish but consolidate his frontrunner position. Some in the media may not yet have caught on to the way the momentum continues to shift, but eventually the reality will sink in.

There are three things Sanders needs to do—and has already started doing in a noticeable way—to move clearly and permanently ahead of Hillary Clinton at the national level: a) dramatic emphasis on minority outreach; b) expansion of his economic message to one of social harmony; and c) delegitimization of the negative populism pervasive in the Republican primary.

Already, Cornel West has given a rousing introduction to Sanders in South Carolina.[1] Sanders has been trying to reach out to the Congressional Black Caucus, though not yet with much luck—but they will come around, once the message becomes clearer. The message is this: Sanders is a much better deal for minorities of every stripe—from embattled African Americans to Hispanics and Asians and others—because of what his policies of economic justice represent compared to the neoliberal repressiveness Clinton and the establishment Democratic Party have to offer.

The Clintons may be very good at talking a good game when it comes to African Americans—Bill, after all, was supposed to be our first black

---
[1] https://www.youtube.com/watch?v=W8cex4VTrwg.

president before the real first black president showed up—but the truth is, and the African American leadership knows it well, that it was Clintonian neoliberalism that really tightened the screws on the African American population by legitimizing extreme income inequality as the normal course of things—smashing, in effect, the Democratic party's bargain with minorities since the New Deal.

The Clintons ended welfare as we knew it, for example, by delusionally hoping that technology-driven productivity would somehow make poverty cease to exist, or by expanding the surveillance, prosecution, and incarceration capacities of the state, building on the war on drugs initiated by Ronald Reagan to impose a stark omnipotence much less forgiving of mistakes made by poor people. Rhetorically—and emptily—the Clintons may align themselves with African Americans, and claim some sort of honorary status with that community, but their policies have been death—literal death on the streets—for African Americans.

It is a myth created by the establishment media that Sanders's appeal is limited to well-educated white coastal liberals, particularly males, and that he has a natural barrier to how far and deep his support can extend. The claim is that South Carolina—and then Nevada with its Hispanic population—will be the firewalls that will break Sanders's momentum if he wins in mostly white Iowa and New Hampshire.

But the truth is that Sanders's potential appeal to minorities is unlimited—unlike Clinton's upper limits due to the nature of her past and present policies and her utter incapacity to enunciate anything real that resonates with people beyond neoliberal micro-platitudes being recycled from the 1990s and 2000s. Therefore, Sanders must—and I'm sure he will, in the coming days—go for broke in reaching out to African Americans, Hispanics, and Asians as their natural candidate, and in the process rewrite the whole script for how the Democratic Party courts its vote banks. New, and unprecedented, promises must be made to shatter the silence around issues that neoliberal candidates have zero interest in highlighting.

Secondly, while it has so far been a necessary and indeed winning strategy for Sanders to emphasize a straightforward recital of agenda items—especially single-payer health care, free college tuition, and a $15 minimum wage[1]—Sanders needs to open this up to a message of

---
[1] Outlined by Jonathan Tasini in *The Essential Bernie Sanders and His Vision for America*,

optimism that reaches well beyond the listing of economic policy items. Britain's Jeremy Corbyn has already shown how to do this.

Of course, these need to continue being hammered into consciousness until they became accepted parts of liberal discourse again (as the necessary antidote to Reaganite social darwinism that we never got from the Democratic party), but I'm sure that Sanders will also figure out a way to connect these policy prescriptions to a radically expansive vision of the good life, part of which must involve reimagining America as an honest and responsible citizen in the world community.

There's a reason why Hillary Clinton—like Tony Blair in Britain—has always been utterly incapable of humor. It is not a character flaw per se, as it wasn't for Blair, but the fact that neoliberalism demands a pure administrative outlook, managing at the margins with faith in private enterprise as the only salvation, that simply does not allow any glimpse of humor—by which I really mean humanity—to peek through.

Young people everywhere are looking for this streak of humanity in an increasingly robotic, unforgiving, rules-based world. I believe that Sanders, despite his age, or perhaps because of it, can lightheartedly tap into his bona fide countercultural heritage to establish new norms for millennial liberal discourse, making a rousing case for old-fashioned liberty based on economic justice.

This is the ideal Martin Luther King, Jr. and other visionaries at the time were beginning to fashion when we got sidelined, for nearly half a century, by an entirely different vision—Nixonian and ruthless and divisive (Donald Trump is playing from the same script). Neoliberals, it should be noted, will continue to indulge in the false bromides of the culture wars when pressed to the wall; they remain immersed in this methodology of false attack and counterattack, rather than seeking the roots of liberty in economic fairness.

Finally, Trump has gifted almost the perfect platform for Sanders to work against: a dark populism rooted in xenophobia and protectionism, a Machiavellian worldview pitting true Americans versus the racially unacceptable other, setting the stage for Sanders's authentic populism, rooted in participatory democracy, to make all the more sense. The contrast with Trump is one big reason why Sanders has had so much resonance.

---

released by Chelsea Green Publishing on Sept. 8, 2015.

Here, Sanders's outreach, such as when he spoke at Liberty University and was introduced by Jerry Falwell, Jr.,[1] is a longer-term investment, and it will be more difficult to gain traction with this voting constituency than with African Americans and other minorities. But fascistic populism of the talk radio variety needs a strong counterweight, which neoliberalism for the past quarter century, coinciding with the rise of the Clintons, has refused to provide.

One way Sanders is correcting this extreme imbalance in the propaganda wars is by correctly insisting on usage of the term "democratic socialist" to describe himself. His actual policies might not be very socialistic, considering the European use of the term, but it's a brilliant move on his part to shift the terrain of discourse away from neoliberal policy contending with neoliberal policy, which would be the case, for example, if Hillary Clinton and Jeb Bush were to duke it out in the end.

The power imbalance, in favor of corporations, has become so extreme that a new vocabulary for building a movement is needed; and note how Barack Obama, because of his lack of access to such a language, never intended to nor succeeded in any way in building a lasting movement for progress and justice.

Since he gained the upper hand in both Iowa and New Hampshire in the last few days, Sanders seems to have quickly shifted gears and opened up his message and vision. Although dramatic gestures are not his style, I think he needs to say and do some unexpected things of a radical nature to place a bet on minorities moving quickly toward him. When that strategy starts clicking, no one in the neoliberal camp will be able to catch him.

If there is a moment in the first debate where Sanders can convey, through humor, the humanity of his vision—a kind of genuine vulnerability we have not seen for at least fifteen years at the national level—he will become invincible from that point on. And never worry, Hillary Clinton will neither try to outdo him on progressive policy nor demonstration of humanity; that is not the way of neoliberals.

---

[1] https://www.youtube.com/watch?v=P_Ns1oyr0pk.

The Brooklyn Debate:
Bernie Sanders Has Irrevocably Altered the Terms of Discourse

What always disappointed me most about President Obama was how he never tried to change the language of politics that had been established in the eight years of the Bush presidency.

From immigration (on which he never articulated a different rhetoric than the punitive law-and-order one put into effect by his predecessor) to civil liberties to war crimes to inequality to health care to race relations to trade, he has kept to the establishment line on all substantive policy issues. That was the thing that most disillusioned me, it crushed me that he wouldn't even try to speak a more progressive language. I didn't expect him to get any results, but if only he had spoken differently I would have forgiven him anything.

And that's where Bernie Sanders has succeeded so brilliantly, exceeding by an astronomical measure what Ralph Nader, for example, managed to accomplish earlier. Nader had to beg, unsuccessfully, to even get on the debating stage with the major candidates. But starting with negligible poll numbers, Sanders has managed to draw level with Hillary Clinton in the national polls, and seriously threatens to upset the carefully balanced apple cart by pulling out a win in New York. As a result, he has pushed the establishment to acknowledge, at least rhetorically, the grievances of the powerless. That is no mean accomplishment, and he and his supporters should feel proud for having come this far.

I do not of course mean this in the dismissive way deployed by Clinton and the rest of the "establishment" (the term Sanders repeatedly uses to describe her and which irks her so much), to pat Sanders and his followers on the back, as if to say, Job well done, now go home and let the adults take over. Indeed, toward the end of the debate tonight, as Clinton became increasingly nervous—her shrill bluster and bravado seemed to have collapsed by the end, as Sanders only seemed to gain in confidence and grit—that is precisely the rhetorical tactic Clinton used against him.

No, it's not going to work now, things have changed, we have moved past the likes of Debbie Wasserman Schultz pushing the debates to ungodly weekend hours, pretending that there was never a split among liberals as severe as that among conservatives.

Once Sanders refused to go after Clinton's email follies in the first debate, I found it unbearable to watch Clinton's arrogance in subsequent debates. As Sanders narrowly lost some key early states, I wondered what would have happened had he been quick to attack from the get-go, but he's an honorable man who believes that better ideas will win the day. In a January debate, Sanders seemed to miss opportunities to call her out on her lies. Clinton is a weak candidate, because her history of neoliberal complicity is at odds with the progressive agenda, and I always thought she was ripe to be taken down in a historic blow to the plutocracy.

Tonight I was shocked by the distance Sanders has traveled in confidence and maturity, the way he handled all of her maddening lies—particularly as she misused his congressional voting record in the absurd way of political commercials—by insisting on the facts.[1] The facts are all we need, but we have not been hearing them on such a visible platform in a long time. President Obama is also beholden to equivocating establishment-speak, which fuzzes up clear-cut issues of unequal treatment and distracts attention to pragmatism and "competence" (of course the neoliberal banker in a politician's suit is the only one who's competent).

I was surprised too at the respect Sanders has gained from an establishment outlet like CNN, with moderator Wolf Blitzer, as well as the two questioners Dana Bash and Errol Louis, being pretty even-handed and going after Clinton to answer the question at hand rather than defaulting into the screaming hand-waving she typically resorts to when she has no defense.

It was a joy to witness the establishment stripped down and denuded. There were actually two other dignitaries—Bill Clinton and Barack Obama—who stood behind Hillary Clinton, on this night when the hypocrisies of the powerful stood exposed on the national stage. Using the kind of hardcore logic and rationality that went out of style after

---

[1] The historic CNN debate between Bernie Sanders and Hillary Clinton, April 14, 2016, can be seen at: https://www.youtube.com/watch?v=KunPfHnefiw.

Walter Mondale's unsuccessful deployment of the same against warm fuzzy Ronald Reagan, but which made a brief appearance when Joe Biden went head to head against Paul Ryan, Sanders didn't let Clinton get away with her prevarications on a single point. And of course she equivocated and feinted right and left and diverted attention and raised false alarms in response to every question.

Clinton attempted to subdue every sharp query that came her way by speaking in praise of the incremental measures she intends to take toward what she has now taken to calling her own "bold" ideas, such as raising the minimum wage in steps by way of getting to the progressive goal of $15 an hour. She mocked the idea of free college by offering her father's homely wisdom that one should "read the fine print" when something is offered for free. But Sanders never gave her a free pass, and neither did the moderators, to their credit. In contrast to previous debates, certainly in recent election cycles, the argument remained firmly grounded in facts rather than distractions, fears, and absurd hypotheticals, which by itself is a notable shift in consciousness.

As the debate wore on, the contradictions in Clinton's attempt to square the circle became more and more evident. Sanders had worn her down so greatly, with the gentlemanly demeanor she so clearly despises, that he had to do less and less work to expose her lies. He would simply shake his head and sputter in disbelief, while Clinton seemed to dig ever deeper holes for herself.

In the name of incrementalist competence, she refused to answer whether she would support a tax on Wall Street speculative transactions (an orthodox economic idea that has been around for decades), couldn't excuse her way out of support for fracking technology around the world, refused to grant that Israel had used "disproportionate response" in answering any attacks, and couldn't find a way to escape from her advocacy of escalated military action in Libya and Syria.

She often fell back on 9/11 and her "response" to it, as a savior of New York. The adults are here to protect us, what does a wide-eyed socialist like Sanders, beholden to European values, even know about managing the economy? Dodd-Frank, that parody of a neoliberal law to save us from the next financial collapse, was Clinton's only resort as the manager who pursues goals strictly through established law. Meanwhile, her absurd charges that Sanders is somehow a supporter of assault weapons or a lover of swaps and derivatives or a threat to Israel fell flat.

This has been the diversionary recourse for conservative democrats for a long time now, but it is not going to work this time, regardless of the outcome of the Democratic nomination and the general election. The genie is well and truly out of the bottle. Sanders's campaign—unlike, say, Jerry Brown's humanist unorthodoxy in 1992—has gone on too long and scored too many points that have hurt the establishment deeply and irrevocably. This is what I gathered from this debate, where the energy—despite Clinton's claims to New York as home turf—was ecstatically on Sanders's side, particularly in his rousing closing statement.

Sanders has stayed on message, a simple one, the only one that matters, of economic inequality and unequivocal ways to address it. Like her predecessors, Clinton has sought to keep the debate focused on the culture wars; she did it again in her closing statement tonight, almost seeming to glide by economic inequality and instead talking about cultural "barriers" to opportunity, the distracting dance that neoliberals like to do at every opportunity. She would never have brought up a single substantive issue during this campaign, following the release of her vacuous self-affirming opening campaign commercial, had Sanders not forced the issue. She is trying her damnedest to speak the progressive lingo for now, until Sanders is put away by the superdelegates or other shenanigans of machine politics at which both Clintons excel, but it doesn't suit her and tonight it was glaringly obvious.

Neoliberalism, from this point on, will not have the cover it did before the Sanders campaign. Future progressive movements will have a firmer foothold to stand on. The fantasy that only neoliberal stalwarts have the competence to handle money and defense has been shattered. Late last year, the question was how—and if—Sanders could get minorities to come over to his side. We are now talking about palpable shifts on every objective measure, and perhaps even the possibility of making his case at the convention. Even if he should fall short of that, the key idea progressives should take from his winning campaign is that the first and most important thing to do is to change the terms of discourse, because to speak in the other side's language is to concede defeat.

It is not a coincidence that it often tends to be people of much earlier generations—like Nader and now Sanders—who bring out the youthfulness in the young. The facts, spoken by the mature and wise, have a way of rousing the listless. The facts, about our distorted policies, are back on the table. In response to why Sanders, at the Apollo theater, called out Bill Clinton for defending his wife against the use of the term "superpredators" in the 1990s, Sanders simply said, "Because it was a racist term, and everybody knew it was a racist term." That is the kind of clear shift in discourse we've needed all along.

The Unraveling of the Two-Party System and the Desperation of the Elites

Looking beyond the daily tussle between Donald J. Trump and the Republican Party, or Bernie Sanders and the Democratic Party, let's consider the larger historical picture to see what the current election campaign tells us about the state of the two major political parties and their future.

Over the last forty years both major political parties have been in a state of terminal decline for a number of reasons, primarily the ideological contradictions each has developed quite in sync with the other, driven by the same economic trends. Both are in a death spiral at the moment, but this being America, where political accountability is not as rapid or conclusive as in Europe, it's likely that they will continue in more or less their existing forms for the foreseeable future, further deepening the crisis of legitimacy. Whatever the realities about their loss of credibility, we are not likely to hear an announcement anytime soon that the Democratic or Republican parties are dead, having ceased to serve the respective functions for which they accumulated much legitimacy at different points in the twentieth century.

It may seem, with stronger party identification over the last couple of decades, that the parties are stronger than ever, but this would be misleading on several counts. The fact most frequently cited in support of the parties' strength is increased polarity in congress, where in recent decades members of each party have moved farther toward the extremes, which means less bipartisan consensus.[1] The electorate has sharply divided, with left and right divisions more pronounced, amidst the now

---

[1] The Brookings Institution has done much good analysis on this, as reported by the *Washington Post* here: https://www.washingtonpost.com/blogs/the-fix/wp/2014/04/14/how-congress-became-more-partisan-over-time-in-four-charts. At present there are no Republican members of congress more liberal than any Democrat, and no Democratic members of congress more conservative than any Republican.

familiar phenomenon of the red state/blue state split which first became prominently visible in the 2000 election.

But it would be a mistake to confuse ideological polarity with party loyalty. In congress, members have no choice but to support the party closest to their ideological leanings, and likewise for the populace at large.[1] Third parties have had a difficult time getting off the ground in America—what should have developed into a breakaway anti-corporate party after the Seattle WTO protests in 1999 and Ralph Nader's candidacy in 2000 never happened—so the lack of party choice at the national level creates the illusion of strong party support.

The last time the establishment—both Republican and Democratic—publicly bemoaned the loss of legitimacy for government, which included the state of the parties, was in the 1970s.[2] This was a persistent theme throughout that decade, after the landslide McGovern defeat in 1972, and the ouster of President Nixon in 1974. An impression was perpetuated by the elites that the U.S. was on the run against communism on all continents.[3] After the 1973 oil embargo, and the stagflation that lasted throughout the decade, Keynesian policy—the glue that had held the New Deal coalition together for decades— swiftly unraveled. The crisis

---

[1] The proportion of self-identified independents, as opposed to self-identified Democrats or Republicans, is at an all-time high, nearly forty percent, according to the most recent Pew report: http://www.people-press.org/2015/04/07/a-deep-dive-into-party-affiliation/.

[2] Represented, for example, by the report *Crisis of Democracy: On the Governability of Democracies*, authored by Michael J. Crozier, Samuel P. Huntington, and Joji Watanuki (Trilateral Commission, 1975), which argued that the crisis of governance arose from too much democracy and that government institutions needed to be relegitimized and strengthened to overcome the crisis; in essence the story of the past forty years is one of implementation of this plan to regather democratic forces and funnel power upward. The full report can be read here:
http://trilateral.org/download/doc/crisis_of_democracy.pdf. Not surprisingly, a new version of this theory, again stemming from the liberal side, arrived with Fareed Zakaria's *The Future of Freedom: Illiberal Democracy at Home and Abroad* (2003).

[3] Prominent neoconservative Jeane Kirkpatrick, for example, made specious distinctions between authoritarian and totalitarian countries, and argued for U.S. support of traditional authoritarian countries to prevent their deliverance, via excessive liberalization, to Marxism. According to Kirkpatrick, "Traditional autocrats do not disturb the habitual rhythms of work and leisure, habitual places of residence, habitual patterns of family and personal relations. Because the miseries of traditional life are familiar, they are bearable to ordinary people who, growing up in the society, learn to cope."

was deep and sustained, both domestically and globally, and the parties and their allied establishments seemed to have their days numbered.

Bizarre and illogical compromises began occurring at that time to preserve the sanctity of the parties, and of the narrow liberal-conservative identification, awkward arrangements that are bearing full fruit only today.

On the Democratic side, President Carter began nudging the party in the direction of corporate, free trade, tight monetarist policies that were later to find their most optimistic rendition during Bill Clinton's administration. The recession of the early 1980s, which coincided with President Reagan's first years, was actually launched by Fed chairman Paul Volcker under a Democratic president.[1] The invasion of Afghanistan by the Soviet Union led the Democratic party down a renewed path of militarism—although during the 1970s and 1980s often by proxy means rather than direct intervention—that reached a crisis point in the late 1990s and early 2000s.[2]

But all this provided only a patchwork solution to the Democratic party's crisis of legitimacy. Was it a pro-corporate (neoliberal) or pro-labor (New Deal) party? The actual tendency was for the party to move firmly in the former direction, while escalating rhetorical claims for the rights of cultural minorities, at the same time as the Republican party moved swiftly toward a neoconservative solution to its own crisis. Meanwhile, the Democrats never really addressed the popular roots of dissatisfaction: in a global economy with more dispersed power, both economic and political, how was the standard of living of the American middle-class to be maintained?

The huge popularity of Bernie Sanders on the left today speaks to precisely this dilemma, fundamentally unaddressed through four decades of deceit and illusion to maintain elite power, as inequality continuously rose in that period of time, the middle class became ever more

---

[1] Milton Friedman's successful monetarist attack on Keynesianism, which fundamentally defines policy to this day, was allowed an easy access point by the failure of the Democratic intellectual elites to stand up for collective action under Keynesian policy; likewise, to this day they remain defenseless against vulgarized interpretations of Friedrich von Hayek's invalidation of collective action, a theory which has burrowed deep into the core of Republican orthodoxy.

[2] Responding to the monstrous toll of hundreds of thousands of dead children due to the sanctions on Iraq, Secretary of State Madeleine Albright famously justified the deaths by saying, "We think the price is worth it."

diminished, and real political power became confined to a vanishingly small elite group.[1]

The Republican establishment, over the last forty years, pursued a parallel, and often intersecting (especially in times of war and recession), path as the Democrats. Although Ronald Reagan didn't make it all the way in 1976, because the wounds from Nixon's ouster were still too raw, their own patchwork coalition—nationalist and militarist, beholden to the myth of the free market and personal responsibility, and committed to pulling back the hard-won social and economic rights of the minorities and the poor—proved to be a winning one for a long time.

It meant that the Republican elites had to put up with a lot of sound and fury about cultural issues like abortion (to feed the evangelical beast), while having a free hand to accumulate the same kind of power, economic and political, within an increasingly smaller elite's exclusive grasp as was the case with the Democrats.

In time, particularly with Bill Clinton's "new democrat" retreat from what remained of the New Deal commitment, the gap between the two establishments narrowed, often to the point of invisibility. Think, for example, of the merger of sensibilities right after 9/11, when Democrats and Republicans unified around reneging on civil liberties and authorizing illegal actions in war and at detention sites. The same unification of the elites occurred in the prelude to the Iraq war, and in the aftermath of the financial collapse. Barack Obama started off being open to a "grand bargain" to further deplete the remaining social safety net in the name of fiscal responsibility, and one can expect Hillary Clinton (like Jeb Bush, had he been the nominee) to be on the hunt for similar grand bargains. Each crisis makes the uniformity between the parties manifest, which riles up the populist base on either side to even greater degrees of frustration.

Trump's heresy is to point out, as he did in a recent debate, that the Iraq war was based on lies, and that George W. Bush did not keep us safe. These are obvious facts, but they are not uttered in Republican elite circles. Jeb Bush, as a result of the truth-telling, and the capacity of the failing middle class to see through the establishment's fog of confusion, stood discredited, as is increasingly the case with Hillary Clinton, whose every defense of Bill Clinton's punitive neoliberal policies on crime and

lxxviiilxxviiilxxviii─────────
[1] Numerous polls suggest that, in the wake of the Sanders campaign, younger Americans are more open to socialism than ever before.

welfare and civil liberties makes her husband's administration transparent as the sordid hodgepodge of concessions to corporate hegemony that it was.[1]

The Republican party can no longer keep its disaffected constituents under control either; under various guises—the silent majority, the Reagan Democrats, the Tea Party, and now the Trumpheads—they have been making their presence felt again and again, though for four decades the party has been able to keep diverting the subject, particularly with national security anxieties. Likewise, the Democrats cannot keep their old faithful on the reservation, who also keep making their anti-corporate sentiments felt, mostly recently with the Occupy movement and the Sanders upsurge. They are the same ones who trusted that Obama would weaken the corporate stronghold, but were quickly disillusioned when he did no such thing; and the ones supporting Trump are generally the same kind of people who went with Ross Perot in an earlier time as he raised hell about NAFTA's impact on American industrial jobs, or with Pat Buchanan as he stoked white nationalist resentments.

I suspect that if the half of the population that doesn't vote were to do so, most of them would fall in line with either Trump or Sanders; these are the ones who are so disillusioned, or disempowered, that they do not even bother to participate. Both parties have long since left them. In this sense too, the statistics cited on behalf of strong party identification, or ideological polarization along strict party lines, are illusionary.

Again and again, the establishment has been able to paper over the underlying crisis of legitimacy with artful means designed to hoodwink people. Reagan's morning in America, Bill Clinton's new economy, George Bush's war on terrorism, Obama's hope and change, and on it goes, with what would have been—and perhaps still will be—Hillary Clinton or Ted Cruz's new social alignment (a further strengthening of the neoliberal wise on what little remains of freedom in America, with a theological veneer in the case of Cruz or rhetorical multiculturalism in the case of Clinton, but with the same overall effect).

This time, however, the people, both on the Democratic and Republican sides, can see through the strategy to divert attention from

lxxviiilxxviiilxxviii————————————

[1] Bill Clinton himself lost it recently when defending Hillary's "superpredators" categorization against Black Lives Matter protestors:
http://www.nydailynews.com/new-york/bill-clinton-defends-hillary-superpredators-comment-article-1.2592451.

the hollowness of American economic and cultural life. It's still a strong bet that the establishment—outmaneuvering Trump and Sanders through the arcane undemocratic operations of delegate allocation—will pull through, for yet another eight years of war and economic misery and curtailment of freedom. The crisis will only fester with more malevolent outpourings slated for the future, until perhaps someone even more dictatorial than Trump comes along.

Had the elites chosen to be more democratic thirty or forty or twenty years ago, both parties would have naturally evolved and reshaped themselves in accord with shifting social and economic realities. Democrats would have been more realistic about the tolls of trade on displaced workers rather than putting their heads in the sand, while Republicans would have applied the notion of limited government to private life rather than limiting it to corporations. Liberalism and conservatism, in their authentic manifestations, would have continued fighting the good fight, rather than the situation that has developed, where economic anxiety is continually suppressed and allowed to manifest only in twisted movements that have little chance of accomplishing any objectives given the present distribution of power.

It is noteworthy that a great many among America's intellectual elite support Hillary Clinton over Bernie Sanders, offering standard neoliberal justifications, whereas those outside elite intellectual circles are more likely to support Sanders; likewise with Trump and his antagonists and supporters.[1] What the establishment will not do is take either of them seriously; meaning that they will not, as they haven't for forty years, acknowledge the concerns of the constituencies they are supposed to represent, and direct the very real anxieties felt on all parts of the political spectrum toward positive resolutions good for the country and for the rest of the world.

---

[1] Trump has recently asserted that if the real economic misery index were not something around twenty percent rather than the official five percent unemployment rate he would not be getting the number of people he does at his rallies; likewise, the elites typically dismiss Sanders's calls for free higher education and health care as unattainable in the richest country in the world; Clinton defender Paul Krugman calls the idealism of Sanders's young followers "petulant self-righteousness."

Five-Alarm Panic in Progress: Should We Listen to the Hypocritical Elites Who Can't Even Own up to Trump?

This week, on the night of the Indiana primary, I read one of the most loathsome political screeds it has been my misfortune to encounter.[1]

It was an alarm bell raised by Andrew Sullivan, arguably the greatest hypocrite of the Bush era, on par with his partner in many crimes Christopher Hitchens (remember "Islamofascism?"). Sullivan proclaims that the election of Trump would be an "extinction-level" event. Well, perhaps it will be.

But the extinction Sullivan is most worried about is clearly that of his own breed of callous elites, who could care less about normal human beings who do not have decent jobs and who live in crappy housing and who are so desperate to find a way out of the trap that even someone like Trump starts sounding rational to them.

Now this panic alert, designed to get us in line behind Hillary, is raised by the man who ended *The New Republic* as we knew it (which then went on to end and then end again), promoting racist and imperialist dogma during his reign at the magazine in the 1990s, and then, with his finger in the wind (which to him and that other arch-hypocrite Hitchens meant being like George Orwell), turned into one of the biggest shills for the war on terror, the Iraq war, the whole works, all the while denouncing the fifth column within our ranks. This so-called journalist, who has no record of liberal consistency, who keeps shifting to whoever holds moral power at any given moment, is scaring us about the mortal threat that is Trump.

No, the danger is the elites, who have made such a joke of the democratic process, who have so perverted and rotted it from within,

---
[1] Andrew Sullivan, "Democracies End When They Are Too Democratic," *New York Magazine*, May 1, 2016: http://nymag.com/daily/intelligencer/2016/04/america-tyranny-donald-trump.html.

that the entire edifice is crumbling (to the consternation of the elites). Both parties are in terminal decline after forty years of ignoring the travails of the average worker (the Republicans admit they're in the intensive care unit, while the Democrats calling for Sanders to quit already have yet to come around to admitting that they might have the flu), and voters on both right and left have at last—and this is a breath of relief—stopped caring about the cultural distractions that have kept the elites in power. No, they want their jobs back, even if it means building a wall, keeping Muslims out, deporting the illegals, and starting trade wars with China and Japan—because what else did the elites give them, they're still opposing a living wage!

Sullivan comes right out and says it: it's all because of *too much democracy*, the same bugbear elites on both sides have been offended by since the "crisis of excess democracy" in the mid-1970s, the same lament that Sullivan's masters in the ivory tower, Samuel P. Huntington and others, have been leveling ever since they made it their job to put the exuberance of the late sixties and early seventies to rest once and for all. So they engineered the neoliberal revolution, where the "qualified" elites are firmly in charge, and the only way to get ahead is not democratic (or individualist) unpredictability—and who is a greater exemplar of unpredictability than Trump?—but elite planning, a certain coldhearted "rationality" that is as efficient as any totalitarian system ever was in sidelining those who do not have what it takes to succeed.

So, the problem, according to all the elites, is *too much democracy*. Thank you Andrew Sullivan, a Harvard humanities education—all that Plato you read!—was hardly ever put to worse use in the four-hundred-year annals of the institution.

You, Andrew Sullivan, and the Democratic party flacks who want the Bernie supporters to throw our lot behind the most compromised Democratic candidate of all time, Hillary Clinton, and you, who are so worried about the wall and the ban on Muslims and the attack on civil liberties, will you please tell us who started it all?

You did!

You've all now, the elite punditocracy on either spectrum, suddenly become nostalgic for George W. Bush, because he didn't—well, not always—use the crude and blatant vocabulary that Trump deploys to demonize Mexicans and Arabs and Muslims and foreigners. But Bush is the one who actually implemented, with your full support, plans to surveil, discriminate against (in immigration proceedings), and impose a de facto bar on Muslims from the "wrong countries" that is still, under Barack Obama, a severe disability on Muslims who may want to emigrate to this country.

Where were you elites when Barack Obama, Hillary Clinton, and the Democratic party elite spoke as one with Republicans on endlessly strengthening border security, on the need to mercilessly enforce immigration laws, on imposing such punitive measures against potential legalization that it becomes possible only in theory not in reality?

The natural conclusion of these ideas is the literal wall, but Trump didn't start it, he's only putting the finishing touches on the discourse that you elites, on both sides, have inflamed for twenty-plus years. Bill Clinton started the demonization of immigrants—*legal* immigrants were made ineligible for benefits—for the first time since the liberalization of immigration laws in 1965. Bill Clinton ended welfare, tapping into racist discourse about African Americans, and permanently unmoored millions of people from the social safety net. No, Trump didn't start any of it, Paul Begala and Karl Rove, representing both parties, and the elite interests they represent, poisoned the discourse.

Elites on both sides insisted on not addressing the root causes of economic dissatisfaction, hence the long-foreseen rise of Trump. Paul Krugman, a Hillary acolyte, is nothing more than a neoliberal, whose prescriptions always stay strictly within orthodox parameters. Yet he was construed as some sort of a liberal lion during the Bush and Obama years. Not for him any of Bernie's "radical" measures to ensure economic justice and fairness. Oh no, we have to stay within the orthodoxies of the economics profession. Now he's all offended about Trump!

The worst offenders of all are the American left's cultural warriors, who daily wage some new battle over some imagined cultural offense, which has nothing to do with the lives of normal people but only the highly tuned sensibilities of those in the academic, publishing, and media ecospheres.

Today, as I write, the controversy is about the venerable *Antioch Review* having micro-offended yet another cultural sensibility,[1] over which the entire literary world is in arms, signing petitions to punish the *Antioch Review*, just as a few weeks ago they were after *The New Yorker* and that

---
[1] Scott Jaschik, "*Antioch Review*'s Editor, Author Respond to Criticism," *Inside Higher Ed.*, May 9, 2016: https://www.insidehighered.com/quicktakes/2016/05/09/antioch-review-editor-author-respond-criticism.

white imperialist racist sexist moron Calvin Trillin who thought it would be funny to write a light-hearted poem about the white bourgeoisie trying to keep up with Asian cuisine. Yes, the *Antioch Review*, which was around to fight fascism—actual fascism, not the Trumpocalypse version of it—back in the dark days of the second world war, and fought the good fight with the power of intelligent words written with passion and conviction.

The Hillary supporters have the authoritarian mentality of small property owners. They are the mirror image of the "realist" Trump supporters, the difference being that the Trump supporters fall below the median income level, and are distressed and insecure, while the Hillary supporters stand above the median income level, and are prosperous but still insecure.

To manipulate them, the Democratic and Republican elites have both played a double game for forty years and have gotten away with it. They have incrementally yet quite comprehensively seized all economic and political power for themselves. They have perverted free media and even such basics of the democratic process as voting and accountability in elections. Elites on both sides have collaborated to engineer a revolution of economic decline for the working person, until the situation has reached unbearable proportions. The stock market may be doing well, and unemployment may theoretically be low, but people can't afford housing and food, they can't pay back student loans and other debts, their lives, wherever they live in this transformed country, are full of such misery that there is not a single word that an establishment candidate like Hillary Clinton or Jeb Bush says that makes sense to them.

When they did have a difference to choose from—i.e., the clear progressive choice, Bernie over Hillary, who consistently demonstrates beating Trump by double the margins Hillary does—the elites went for Hillary, even though she poses the greater risk of inaugurating Trump as president. And now you want us to listen to your panic alarms?

The game, for the elites, is over. This is true no matter what happens with the Sanders campaign. The Republican party as we have known it since the Reagan consensus (dating back to 1976) is over. The Democratic party doesn't know it yet, but Bill Clinton's neoliberalism (and what followed in his wake with complicity with Bush junior, and the continuation of Bush junior's imperialist policies with Barack Obama) is also over, or well on its way to being over. The elites are in a cataclysmic state of panic, they don't know whether to look right or left, they have no idea what to do with Trump, they don't know what to do with the Bernie diehards, they have no idea how to put Humpty Dumpty together again.

And these same elites, both liberal and conservative, these same journalists and celebrities, became quite comfortable with Bush once the war on terror was on. They'll get used to Trump too, his level of fascist escalation will soon be presented by *The Times* and other institutions as something our democracy can handle, just as they continually assured us during those eight years of gloom that our democracy could easily take care of Bush. We, the citizens, don't need to get our hands dirty with implementing checks and balances, the elites will do it on our behalf. Soon, once he starts talking to the elites, you won't even be that afraid of Trump. Wait, he's the one who wants to make America great again, and what's so wrong with that?

The election of Trump would end the Republican party as we know it, but more refreshingly it would also end the Democratic party as we know it. The limits of the academic left's distracting cultural discourse in keeping economic dissatisfaction in check would be fully exposed. Trump threatens the stability of the fearmongering discourse of Sullivan and his like. The threat to their monopoly of discourse is the real reason for the panic.

Oh, and Hillary, good luck fighting Trump with your poll-tested reactions. Your calculated "offenses" against his offensiveness against women or minorities or Muslims are going to be as successful as the sixteen Republicans who've already tried it. You won't be able to take on Trump because you do not speak the truth, you speak only elite mumbo-jumbo. Trump doesn't speak the truth either, but he's responding to something in the air that has an element of truth, and you don't even go that far, you speak to a state of affairs—a meritocratic, democratic, pluralist America—that doesn't even exist.

What, Exactly, Is Neoliberalism?
And Why We Should Care Beyond the Current Election Campaign

Over the last fifteen years as I wrote for many progressive outlets, editors often asked me not to mention the word "neoliberalism," because I was told readers wouldn't comprehend the "jargon." The situation is even worse with literary journals, my main territory, which are determined not to have anything to do with this vocabulary. This has begun to change recently, as the terminology has come into wider usage, though it remains shrouded in great mystery.

People throw the term around loosely, as they do with "fascism," with the same confounding results. Imagine living under fascism or communism, or earlier, classical liberalism, and not being allowed to acknowledge that particular frame of reference to understand economic and social issues. Imagine living under Stalin and never using the communist framework but focusing only on personality clashes between his lieutenants, or likewise for Hitler or Mussolini or Mao or Franco and their ideological systems! But this curious silence, this looking away from ideology, is exactly what has been happening for a quarter century, since neoliberalism, already under way since the early 1970s, got turbocharged by the Democratic party under the Democratic Leadership Council (DLC) and Bill Clinton.[1] We live under an ideology that has not been widely named or defined!

Absent the neoliberal framework, we simply *cannot* grasp what is good or bad for citizens under Cruz versus Trump, or Clinton versus Sanders, or Clinton versus Trump, away from the distraction of personalities. To what extent does each of them agree or disagree with neoliberalism? Are there important differences? How much is Sanders a deviation? Can we still rely on conventional distinctions like liberal versus conservative, or

---

[1] Alex Chadwick, "Hillary Clinton to Chart Centrist Democratic Agenda," *NPR*, July 26, 2005: http://www.npr.org/templates/story/story.php?storyId=4771471.

Democrat versus Republican, to understand what is going on? How do we grasp movements like the Tea Party, Occupy, and now the Trump and Sanders insurgencies?

Neoliberalism has been more successful than most past ideologies in redefining subjectivity, in making people alter their sense of themselves, their personhood, their identities, their hopes and expectations and dreams and idealizations. Classical liberalism was successful too, for two and a half centuries, in people's self-definition, although communism and fascism succeeded less well in realizing the "new man."

It cannot be emphasized enough that neoliberalism is *not* classical liberalism, or a return to a purer version of it, as is commonly misunderstood; it is a *new* thing, because the market, for one thing, is not at all free and untethered and dynamic in the sense that classical liberalism idealized it. Neoliberalism presumes a strong state, working only for the benefit of the wealthy, and as such it has little pretence to neutrality and universality, unlike the classical liberal state.

I would go so far as to say that neoliberalism is the final completion of capitalism's long-nascent project, in that the desire to transform *everything*—every object, every living thing, every fact on the planet—in its image had not been realized to the same extent by any preceding ideology. Neoliberalism happens to be the ideology—unlike the three major forerunners in the last 250 years—that has the fortune of coinciding with technological change on a scale that makes its complete penetration into every realm of being a possibility for the first time in human history.

From the early 1930s, when the Great Depression threatened the classical liberal consensus (the idea that markets were self-regulating, and the state should play no more than a night-watchman role), until the early 1970s, when global instability including currency chaos unraveled it, the democratic world lived under the Keynesian paradigm:[1] markets were understood to be inherently unstable, and the interventionist hand of government, in the form of countercyclical policy, was necessary to make capitalism work, otherwise the economy had a tendency to get out of whack and crash.

It's an interesting question if it was the stagflation of the 1970s, following the unhitching of the United States from the gold standard and

---

[1] A short primer on Keynesianism:
http://www.economicshelp.org/blog/6801/economics/keynesian-economics/.

the arrival of the oil embargo, that brought on the neoliberal revolution, with Milton Friedman discrediting fiscal policy and advocating a by-the-numbers monetarist policy,[1] or if it was neoliberalism itself, in the form of Friedmanite ideas that the Nixon administration was already pursuing, that made stagflation and the end of Keynesianism inevitable.

It should be said that neoliberalism thrives on prompting crisis after crisis, and has proven more adept than previous ideologies at exploiting these crises to its benefit, which then makes the situation worse, so that each succeeding crisis only erodes the power of the working class and makes the wealthy wealthier. There is a certain self-fulfilling aura to neoliberalism, couched in the jargon of economic orthodoxy, that has remained immune from political criticism, because of the dogma that was perpetuated—by Margaret Thatcher and her acolytes—that There Is No Alternative (TINA).[2]

Neoliberalism is excused for the crises it repeatedly brings on—one can think of a regular cycle of debt and speculation-fueled emergencies in the last forty years, such as the developing country debt overhang of the 1970s,[3] the savings and loan crisis of the 1980s,[4] the Asian currency crisis of the 1990s,[5] and the subprime mortgage crisis of the 2000s—better than any ideology I know of. This is partly because its very existence as ruling ideology is not even noted by the population at large, which continues to derive some residual benefits from the welfare state inaugurated by Keynesianism but has been led to believe by neoliberal ideologues to think of their reliance on government as worthy of provoking guilt, shame, and melancholy, rather than something to which they have legitimate claim.

---

lxxviiilxxviiilxxviii————————————

[1] Milton Friedman's *Capitalism and Freedom* (1962) and *Free to Choose* (1980) are essential to understanding today's ideological landscape. Here he is dissing an idealistic student at Stanford University: https://www.youtube.com/watch?v=0E-URmNAa5o.
[2] The last British Prime Minister, David Cameron, reiterates TINA: https://www.youtube.com/watch?v=r0k4QkVOMNs.
[3] Jerome Roos, "Since the Mexican Debt Crisis, 30 Years of Neoliberalism," *Roar Magazine*, Aug. 22, 2012.
[4] Kimberly Amadeo, "Savings and Loans Crisis: Causes, Cost," *The Balance*, updated September 8, 2016: https://www.thebalance.com/what-is-firrea-3305839.
[5] Ramon Moreno, "What Caused East Asia's Financial Crisis," Federal Reserve Bank of San Francisco, August 7, 1998: http://www.frbsf.org/economic-research/publications/economic-letter/1998/august/what-caused-east-asia-financial-crisis/.

It is not surprising to find neoliberal multiculturalists—comfortably established in the academy[1]—likewise demonizing, or othering, not Muslims, Mexicans, or African Americans, but working-class whites (the quintessential Trump proletariat) who have a difficult time accepting the fluidity of self-definition that goes well with neoliberalism, something that we might call the market capitalization of the self.

George W. Bush's useful function was to introduce necessary crisis into a system that had grown too stable for its own good; he injected desirable panic, which served as fuel to the fire of the neoliberal revolution. Trump is an apostate—at least until now—in desiring chaos on terms that do not sound neoliberal, which is unacceptable; hence Jeb Bush's characterization of him as the "candidate of chaos."[2] Neoliberalism *loves* chaos, that has been its modus operandi since the early 1970s, but only the kind of chaos it can direct and control.

To go back to origins, the Great Depression only ended conclusively with the onset of the second world war, after which Keynesianism had the upper hand for thirty-five years. But just as the global institutions of Keynesianism, specifically the IMF and the World Bank, were being founded at the New Hampshire resort of Bretton Woods in 1944, the founders of the neoliberal revolution, namely Friedrich Hayek, Ludwig von Mises, Milton Friedman, and others were forming the Mount Pelerin Society (MPS) at the eponymous Swiss resort in 1947,[3] creating the ideology which eventually defeated Keynesianism and gained the upper hand during the 1970s.

So what exactly is neoliberalism, and how is it different from classical liberalism, whose final manifestation came under Keynesianism?

Neoliberalism believes that markets are self-sufficient unto themselves, that they do not need regulation, and that they are the best guarantors of human welfare. Everything that promotes the market, i.e., privatization, deregulation, mobility of finance and capital, abandonment of government-provided social welfare, and the reconception of human beings as human capital, needs to be encouraged, while everything that supposedly diminishes the market, i.e., government services, regulation,

---

[1] Michael Kreiter, "Neoliberal Multiculturalism: The Diversity That Divides Us," unpublished paper 2013, Department of Sociology, Boise State University.
[2] https://www.youtube.com/watch?v=vnjv5_rIPeU.
[3] Mount Pelerin Society, "Statement of Aims," originally published April 8, 1947: https://www.montpelerin.org/statement-of-aims/.

restrictions on finance and capital, and conceptualization of human beings in transcendent terms, is to be discouraged.

When Hillary Clinton frequently retorts—in response to demands for reregulation of finance, for instance—that we have to abide by "the rule of law," this reflects a particular understanding of the law, the law as embodying the sense of the market, the law after it has undergone a revolution of reinterpretation in purely economic terms. In this revolution of the law persons have no status compared to corporations, nation-states are on their way out, and everything in turn dissolves before the abstraction called the market.

One way to sum up neoliberalism is to say that everything—*everything*—is to be made over in the image of the market, including the state, civil society, and of course human beings. Democracy becomes reinterpreted as the market, and politics succumbs to neoliberal economic theory, so we are speaking of the end of democratic politics as we have known it for two and a half centuries. As the market becomes an abstraction, so does democracy, but the real playing field is somewhere else, in the realm of actual economic exchange—which is *not*, however, the market. We may say that all exchange takes place on the neoliberal surface.

Neoliberalism is often described—and this creates a lot of confusion—as "market fundamentalism," and while this may be true for neoliberalism's self-promotion and self-presentation, i.e., the market as the ultimate and only myth, as were the gods of the past, I would argue that in neoliberalism *there is no such thing as the market* as we have understood it from previous ideologies.

The neoliberal state—actually, to utter the word state seems insufficient here, I would claim that a new entity is being created, which is not the state as we have known it, but an existence that incorporates potentially all the states in the world and is something that exceeds their sum—is all-powerful, it seeks to leave no space for individual self-conception in the way that classical liberalism, and even communism and fascism to some degree, were willing to allow.

There are competing understandings of neoliberal globalization, when it comes to the question of whether the state is strong or weak compared to the primary agent of globalization, i.e., the corporation, but I am taking this logic further, I am suggesting that the issue is not how strong the state is in the service of neoliberalism, but whether there is anything left over beyond the new definition of the state. Another way to say it is that the state has become the market, the market has become the state, and therefore both have ceased to exist in the form we have classically understood them.

Of course the word hasn't gotten around to the people yet, hence all the confusion about whether Hillary Clinton is more neoliberal than Barack Obama, or whether Donald Trump will be less neoliberal than Hillary Clinton. The project of neoliberalism—i.e., the redefinition of the state, the institutions of society, and the self—has come so far along that neoliberalism is almost beyond the need of individual entities to make or break its case. Its penetration has gone too deep, and none of the democratic figureheads that come forward can fundamentally question its efficacy.

I said almost. The reason why Bernie Sanders, self-declared democratic socialist, is so threatening to neoliberalism is that he has articulated a conception of the state, civil society, and the self that is not founded in the efficacy and rationality of the market. He does not believe—unlike Hillary Clinton—that the market can tackle climate change or income inequality or unfair health and education outcomes or racial injustice, all of which Clinton propagates. Clinton's impending "victory" (whatever machinations were involved in engineering it) will only strengthen neoliberalism, as the force that couldn't be defeated even when the movement was as large and transcendent as Sanders's. Although Sanders doesn't specify "neoliberalism" as the antagonist, his entire discourse presumes it.

Likewise, while Trump supporters want to take their rebellion in a fascist direction, their discomfort with the logic of the market is as pervasive as in the Sanders camp, and is an advance, I believe, over the debt and unemployment melancholy of the Tea Party, the shame that was associated with that movement's loss of identity as bourgeois capitalists in an age of neoliberal globalization. The Trump supporters, I believe, are no longer driven by shame, as was true of the Tea Party, and as has been true of the various dissenting movements within the Republican party, evangelical or otherwise, in the recent past. Rather, they have taken the shackles off and are ready for a no-holds barred "politically incorrect" fight with all others: they want to be "winners," even at the cost of exterminating others, and that is not the neoliberal way, which doesn't acknowledge that there can be winners and losers in the neoliberal hyperspace.

In the current election campaign, Hillary Clinton has been the most perfect embodiment of neoliberalism among all the candidates, she is almost its all-time ideal avatar, and I believe this explains, even if not articulated in such a fashion, the widespread discomfort among the populace toward her ascendancy. People can perceive that her ideology is founded on a conception of human beings striving relentlessly to become human capital (as her opening campaign commercial[1] so overtly depicted), which means that those who fail to come within the purview of neoliberalism should be rigorously ostracized, punished, and excluded.

This is the dark side of neoliberalism's ideological arm (a multiculturalism founded on human beings as capital), which is why this project has become increasingly associated with suppression of free speech and intolerance of those who refuse to go along with the kind of identity politics neoliberalism promotes.

And this explains why the 1990s saw the simultaneous and absolutely parallel rise, under the Clintons, of both neoliberal globalization and various regimes of neoliberal disciplining, such as the shaming and exclusion of former welfare recipients (every able-bodied person *should* be able to find work, therefore under TANF welfare was converted to a performance management system designed to enroll everyone in the workforce, even if it meant below-subsistence wages or the loss of parental responsibilities,[2] all of it couched in the jargon of marketplace incentives).

The actual cost to the state of the AFDC program was minimal, but its symbolism was incalculable. The end of welfare went hand in hand with the disciplinary "crime bill" pushed by the Clintons, leading to an epidemic of mass incarceration. Neoliberalism, unlike classical liberalism, does not permit a fluidity of self-expression as an occasional participant in the market, and posits prison as the only available alternative for anyone not willing to conceive of themselves as being present fully and always in the market.

I believe that the generation of people—in their forties or older—supporting Hillary have already internalized neoliberal subjectivity, which they like to frame as realism or pragmatism, refusing for instance to accept that free college or health care are even theoretical possibilities. After all, they have maintained a measure of success in the past three or

lxxviiilxxviiilxxviii————————————————

[1] https://www.youtube.com/watch?v=N708P-A45D0.
[2] Danilo Trisi and Ladonna Pavetti, "TANF Weakening As a Safety Net for Poor Families," Center on Budget and Policy Priorities, May 14, 2012.

four decades after conceptualizing themselves as marketplace agents. Just as the Tea Party supporters found it intolerable that government should help irresponsible homeowners by bailing them out of unsustainable debt, the Clinton supporters hold essentially the same set of beliefs toward those who dare to think of themselves outside the discipline of the market.

I spoke of the myth of the market, as something that has no existence in reality, because none of the elements that would have to exist for a market to work are actually in place; this is even more true for neoliberalism than it was for the self-conscious annihilation of the market by communism, because at least in that system the market, surreptitiously, as in various Eastern European countries, kept making an appearance. But when the market takes neoliberal shape, i.e., the classical conceptions of the buyer and seller as free agents are gone, then radical inequality is the natural outcome. And inequality in the last four decades, as statistics for the U.S. and everywhere neoliberalism has made inroads prove beyond a doubt,[1] has exploded, thereby invalidating neoliberalism's greatest claim to legitimacy, that it brings about a general increase in welfare. So neoliberalism, to the extent that the inequality discourse has made itself manifest recently, must insist all the more vocally on forms of social recognition, what Clinton, for example, likes to call the "fall of barriers."

Neoliberalism likes to focus on public debt—in the Clinton years debt reduction became a mania, though George W. Bush promptly spent all the accumulated surpluses on tax cuts for the wealthy and on wars of choice—rather than inequality, because the only way to address inequality is through a different understanding of public debt; inequality can only be addressed through higher taxation, which has by now been excluded from the realm of acceptable discourse—except when Sanders, Trump, or Jeremy Corbyn in England go off script.

So to recapitulate neoliberalism's comprehensive success, let us note that we have gone from a liberal, Keynesian, welfare state to a neoliberal, market-compliant, disciplinary state.

Neoliberalism expects—and education at every level has been redesigned to promote this—that economic decision-making will be applied to all areas of life (parenthood, intimacy, sexuality, and identity in

---
[1] Oxfam International, "Richest 1% will own more than all the rest by 2016," Jan. 19, 2015.

any of its forms), and that those who do not do so will be subject to discipline. Everyone must invest in their own future, and not pose a burden to the state or anyone else, otherwise they will be refused recognition as human beings.

This supposed economic "rationality" (though it is the greatest form of irrationality) applies to civil society as much as the state, so that none of the ideals of classical liberalism, or previous ideologies rooted in humanism, are valid any longer, the only value is the iteration of the market (as myth, not reality); in other words, neoliberalism, unlike the elevation of the individual in classical liberalism or the state in fascism or the collectivity in communism, has erected something, the market, that has no real existence, as the only god to serve! And it is just like a god, with an ethereal, unchallengeable, irrefutable, ubiquitous presence. Whatever in state policy does not serve market-conformity is to be banned and banished from memory (the secular scriptures are to be rewritten), which explains neoliberalism's radical narrowing of public discourse, including the severance of identity politics from any class foundation.

Neoliberalism will continue to perpetuate reduced opportunity, because one of its characteristics—as in any system that wants to thrive on the world stage—is to constantly refine the field upon which the human subject can operate.

As such, those displaced workers who have suffered the most from the erosion of the old industries in the former manufacturing centers of the world are not even factors to contend with, they are invisible and cannot be part of the policy equation. To the extent that their actual presence is reckoned with, the economy can be said to have crashed; but the problem doesn't arise because of the management of unemployment or underemployment statistics, unlike a housing crash which is palpable and cannot escape statistical definition.

The danger for neoliberalism—as is clear from the support of millions of displaced human beings for Trump—is that with each crisis neoliberalism sheds more workers, makes individuals and firms more "disciplined," narrows the scope of opportunity even further. At times, the disciplining of the non-neoliberal other—as with the killing of Michael Brown or Eric Garner—explodes to surface consciousness in an unsavory way, so an expert manager like Clinton or Obama is required to tamp down the emotions of such unruly entities as Black Lives Matter which arise in response. If climate change, according to Clinton and her cohort, can and should have market solutions, then surely racial disparity, or police violence, should also have market solutions and no others; it is here that neoliberal multiculturalism, operating in the academy, is so insidious, because at the elite level it functions to validate market discourse, it does not step outside it.

The present breakdown of both major political parties can be explained by the frustration that has built up in the body politic over the past decade, because after the crash there was no sustained intellectual movement to question the myth of the market. The substitution of economic justice with identity politics is something Ralph Nader, Howard Dean, and now Bernie Sanders have contested in a humane manner, while the same process is at work, admittedly in an inhumane way, in the Trump phenomenon.

Thus, also, Hillary Clinton's animus against free college education;[1] that form of expansion of opportunity, which was a reality from the 1950s to the 1980s, cannot be allowed to return, human beings are supposed to invest in their own future earnings potential, they are not entitled to a transcendent experience without barriers manifesting in discipline and self-correction. Education, like everything else, including one's own health, becomes an expensive consumer good, not a right, no longer an experience that might lead to a consciousness beyond the market but something that should be fully encapsulated by the market. If one is a capable market player, education as we have classically understood it becomes redundant.

Unlike the interregnum between 1945-1973, the rising tide—no matter the befuddlements Arthur Laffer and his fellow Reaganite ideologues proffered[2]—does *not* lift all boats today, it is outside the logic of neoliberalism that it do so, so the idea of reforming neoliberalism, or what is often called "globalization with a human face," is a rhetorical distraction. All of the policy innovations—interpreted as "socialism" by the Tea Partiers—offered by Barack Obama fall within the purview of neoliberalism, above all the Affordable Care Act, whose genesis was hatched in neoliberal think tanks decades ago.[3]

lxxviiilxxviiilxxviii───────────────

[1] https://www.youtube.com/watch?v=BZxVjhXC0Bs.
[2] Pamela Prah, "Laffer's Supply-Side Economics Staging a Comeback," *Stateline*/Pew Charitable Trust, March 2, 2012: http://www.pewtrusts.org/en/research-and-analysis/blogs/stateline/2012/03/06/laffers-supplyside-economics-staging-a-comeback
[3] Avik Roy, "How the Heritage Foundation, a Conservative Think Tank, Promoted the Individual Mandate," *Forbes*, October 20, 2011:

It is important to note that neoliberal economic restructuring necessarily means social restructuring, i.e., a movement toward disciplinarity and away from liberalism; the disciplinarity can take a Bushian, Clintonian, or Trumpian form, but these are manifestations of the same tendency.

When wage growth is decoupled from economic growth[1] (as it has been since Friedman and others inaugurated the revolution in the early 1970s), this means that the human subject is ripe for discipline. Furthermore, wage fairness cannot be rationally discussed (hence the obfuscation surrounding the $15 minimum wage orchestrated by Clinton and others) because the concept of the market has been disembedded from society; the market as abstraction, not a concrete reality, makes any notion of reform or restructuring impossible. Like the minimum wage, something like free child care also remains outside the bounds of discourse, because public policy cannot accommodate discussions that do not take the self-regulating market as unassailable myth.

What neoliberalism *can* accommodate is relentless tax cuts (Trump has already offered his huge tax cut plan, as Bush did as his first order of business), which only exacerbate the problem, leading to increasing concentrations of wealth. It has to be said, though, that Ted Cruz more comfortably fit the neoliberal paradigm, with his familiar calls for lower taxes along with reduced regulation and further limits on social welfare, whereas Trump shows, for now, some elements of apostasy. If neoliberalism were to get a Cruz, it would have no problem working with him, or rather, Cruz would have had no problem executing neoliberalism, beyond the surface dissimilarities from Hillary Clinton.

As Sanders has consistently noted,[2] economic inequality leads to political inequality, which means that democracy, after a certain point, becomes only theoretical (viz. *Citizens United* and the electoral influence of such powerful entities as the Koch brothers). Both processes— economic inequality and political inequality—have accelerated after each downturn in the forty-five-year history of neoliberalism, therefore a downturn is always exciting, and even preordained, for a Bush, a Trump, or a Clinton. Again, economic inequality and political polarity (polarity is

---

http://www.forbes.com/sites/theapothecary/2011/10/20/how-a-conservative-think-tank-invented-the-individual-mandate/#2c5410f1621b.
[1] Economic Policy Institute, "The Productivity-Pay Gap," updated Aug. 2016: http://www.epi.org/productivity-pay-gap/.
[2] https://www.youtube.com/watch?v=dTiPr90jk-o.

simply a manifestation of democracy having become dysfunctional) strongly correlate, and both have come to a head in this election.

Neoliberalism's task, from this point on, is to mask and manage the increasing inequalities that are likely to befall humanity, especially as the planet reaches a crisis point in its health.[1] In a way, George W. Bush threw a wrench—he was a perverted Keynesian in a way, believing in war to prime the pump, or inflating unsustainable bubbles, or spending exorbitantly on grandiose gestures—into the process of neoliberal globalization that was going very smoothly indeed under Bill Clinton and would likely have flourished under Al Gore as well. With Hillary Clinton, the movement will be toward further privatization of social welfare, "reforming" it along market principles, as has been true of every neoliberal avatar, whether it was Bill Clinton's incentives to work in the performance management makeover of welfare, George Bush's proposed private social security accounts, Mitt Romney's proposed private health care accounts, or the school vouchers that tempt all of them from time to time.

What remains to be seen is the extent to which the millennial generation might be capable of thinking outside the neoliberal paradigm, i.e., they don't just want more of what neoliberal promises to give them yet fails to deliver, but want things that neoliberalism does not or cannot promise. On this rests the near-term future of the neoliberal project.

Beyond Sanders himself, the key question is the ability of the millennial generation to conceive of themselves outside the neoliberal subjectivity they have been pushed to internalize. They have been encouraged to think of themselves as capital producers, turning their intellectuality into social media popularity for the benefit of capital, in the service of the same abstract market that has no place, no role, no definition beyond the fallen liberal calculus. Does the millennial generation believe, even about its most intimate core, that *everything has been privatized?*

I am not necessarily making a pessimistic prediction. I am merely outlining the strength of an opponent that has refused to be *named* for forty-five years, although it has been the ruling ideology that long! In defining neoliberalism, I have sought to distance myself from the distraction of personalities, and tried to expose the dark side of our

---

[1] The Ayn Rand Institute offers, in all seriousness, a "free-market solution" to climate change: https://www.youtube.com/watch?v=ZkobdaR9wBk.

politics which we can only see when we name and understand the ideology as such. We are up against a system that is so strong that it has survived, for the most part, the last crash, as citizens couldn't get their heads around the idea of nationalizing banks or health care.

It is existentially imperative to ponder what happens beyond Sanders, because neoliberalism has its end-game in sight, letting inequality continue to escalate past the crash point (meaning the point where the economy works for most people), past any tolerable degradation of the planet (which is being reconceptualized in the shape of the market).

What, indeed, does happen beyond Sanders, because as we have seen Hillary Clinton is one of the founders of neoliberal globalization, one of its central historical figures (having accelerated the warehousing of the poor, the attack on trade unions, and the end of welfare and of regulatory prowess), while Trump is an authoritarian figure whose conceptions of the state and of human beings within the state are inconsistent with the surface frictionlessness neoliberalism desires? To go back to Hillary Clinton's opening campaign commercial, to what extent will Americans continue to believe that the self must be entrepreneurially leveraged toward maximum market gains, molded into mobile human capital ever ready to serve the highest bidder?

As to whether a non-neoliberal globalization is possible and what that might look like on the international stage after a quarter-century of Clinton, Bush, and Obama—which is essentially the frustration Trump is tapping into—I'll take that up in a follow-up essay, which will further clarify the differences between Sanders versus Clinton, and Trump versus Clinton.

For now, I would suggest that it is not that globalization causes or has caused neoliberalism, but that neoliberalism has pushed a certain form of globalization that suits its interests. This is a crucial distinction, on which everything else hinges. The neoliberal market doesn't actually exist; at the moment it is pure abstraction; what is actually filling up economic and political space can only be discussed when we step away from this abstraction, as Sanders has so ably done, and as the Occupy and Black Lives Matter movements tentatively set in motion.

Feminists, Stop Obfuscating:
Hillary Clinton Does *Not* Represent Values That Help Women

> "I strongly argued that we had to change the [welfare] system...I didn't think it was fair that one single mother improvised to find child care and got up early every day to get to work while another stayed home and relied on welfare...The third bill passed by Congress cut off most benefits to legal immigrants, imposed a five-year lifetime limit on federal welfare benefits, and maintained the status quo on monthly benefit limits, leaving the states free to set benefit limits...I agreed that he [Bill] should sign it and worked hard to round up votes for its passage...Weeks after Bill signed the law, Peter Edelman and Mary Jo Bane, another friend and Assistant Secretary at HHS who had worked on welfare reform, resigned in protest."
> — Hillary Clinton in her 2003 memoir *Hard Choices*.

Not liking Hillary has nothing to do with her being a woman. It has everything to do with the hypermasculine values she espouses.

Hillary is that rare combination, even in our grotesque political landscape, of a smooth-talking neoliberal with the worst tendencies of a warrior-neoconservative. You couldn't say that about Bill to the same extent, but there isn't a regime change opportunity, a chemical or conventional arms deal, an escalated aerial (or lately drone) war, or an authoritarian friend in need, that Hillary hasn't liked. If we get her, we will only be setting back feminism by decades, because her policies—like welfare "reform"—have always come packaged under the false rubric of caring for women and children.[1] It's like George W. Bush's "compassionate conservatism," the rhetorical cover she needs to enact policies, time after time, that erode women's and children's standing even as she claims to be their steadfast advocate.

It has been disheartening for me to read some female intellectuals, particularly in the New York literary world, rage against any criticism of Hillary. We are told it's only sexism that makes us speak. We'd better

---

[1] Joshua Holland, "How Bill Clinton's Welfare 'Reform' Created a System Rife with Racial Biases," *Moyers & Company*, May 12, 2014.

check our feminist credentials. Are we, who criticize Hillary, misogynists? Then why do we have kind words for, say, Elizabeth Warren?

We've had similar criticisms of Condoleezza Rice, Sarah Palin, and Carly Fiorina. Fiorina, for me, was the scariest person running for president this cycle; you felt that poor autistic Ben Carson, if you begged and pleaded with him for your life, just might spare you, but not Carly! Carly even made a virtue of dragging Hewlett Packard down into the pits, which is not much different than Hillary's indifference to the erosion that occurred in foreign policy during her tenure as Secretary of State, as she failed to move into a more liberal paradigm, insisting on sanctions and other punitive regimes, in countries like Iran, that disproportionately hurt women. John Kerry, once he took over, quickly picked up the dropped ball and achieved diplomatic success on a range of fronts, including climate change, where Hillary had failed.

There is a palpable deficit of feminist values in this country's politics, after sixteen dark years of war, surveillance, vigilantism, police controls, economic servitude, and debt. To the extent that we can generalize about feminine and masculine values, the country desperately desires—well, two-thirds of it anyway, those besides Trump and Cruz fans—a reinjection of feminine values. That means compassion, acceptance, and understanding for those left behind by misguided economic policies. That means valuing, once again, as this nation has done for the periods it has shone brightest, imagination, beauty, soft-spokenness, and unexpected generosity.

In the early 1990s Hillary did represent, to some limited symbolic level, a change for the better in terms of feminist values—though this certainly didn't translate into actual policy improvements for women or children or minorities, rather the opposite occurred in policies engineered by the Clintons. Furthermore, one could argue that it was George H. W. Bush who prompted the relative humanization of the 1990s, after the harsh Reagan-era rhetoric, promising a kindler, gentler nation, and aspiring to be the "education president" and "the environmental president." The elder Bush's policies were to the left of either Clinton, when it came to immigration, civil liberties, clean air, disability, and many other issues.

The Clintons went out of their way to pursue—often gratuitously—policies that hurt women and children. The reelection seemed safely in their pockets, yet they went ahead anyway with harmful laws on crime, welfare, telecommunications, immigration, and surveillance, legitimizing right-wing discourse that was to bear full fruit in the following decade. It was the Clintons who set the stage for the massive harm that was to befall women, immigrants, the poor, the elderly, and children once they provided liberal cover to social darwinist ideas that had been swirling around in maniacal think tanks but had not been able to make it through congress.

The Clintons have somehow managed to convince half the sane world that they should be the natural recipients of African-American votes, despite everything they have done, when in power, to erode the economic security of African Americans and other minorities; the false hope raised during the 1990s was that the economic boom, itself a mirage as it turned out, would eventually lead to significant wage gains, but that never happened.

Poor and minority women and children were drastically hurt by the welfare bill the Clintons so enthusiastically pushed through congress, and likewise all the policies, from trade to student aid, they pursued in the name of fiscal responsibility, cutting the deficit and the debt, and playing by Wall Street's tune. On neoliberal disciplinary virtues (which in Hillary's mouth are twisted in a rhetoric of "empowerment"), she's little different than Milton Friedman,[1] the greatest post-war popularizer of the "free market" mythos. "Personal responsibility," separating the virtuous from those deserving of sanctions, is as much a credo for her as it was for Reagan, as it was for Barry Goldwater.

The global IMF and World Bank consensus, the regime of structural adjustment to make developing countries fall in line with the diktat of bankers in the developed world, reached the peak of its authority during the 1990s (even Reagan hadn't been as effective at legitimizing the paradigm in the developing world). The so-called "Washington consensus" was, and remains, a nihilistic retort to any type of redistributive policies poorer countries might wish to pursue to uplift their people.[2] Is cutting education and health care and utility subsidies, in the name of balancing budgets to the satisfaction of the global banking elite, a feminist value? Yet no one is more responsible than the Clintons for making the withdrawal of government from public services

lxxviiilxxviiilxxviii—————————————

[1] Milton Friedman discusses why welfare is a "failure": https://www.youtube.com/watch?v=bROcMAdZT9c.
[2] Women's Environment and Development Organization, "Shortchanging Women: How U.S. Economic Policy Impacts Women Worldwide": http://www.wedo.org/wp-content/uploads/shortchanging-women-factsheet.pdf.

worldwide gospel—at least until some Latin American countries finally started breaking away from the imposition in the 2000s.

Though she still likes to present herself as a fighter for women's and children's rights, let's keep our sights on Hillary's actual record.

When Central American refugee children started streaming over the southern border a couple of years ago, Hillary was quick on the mark to condemn these poor souls to death and oppression. In a 2014 discussion with Christiane Amanpour,[1] she refused to say that she would allow *unaccompanied minors* fleeing violence to stay in the country, insisting instead on the "message" of deterrence that had to be sent to prevent others from thinking of seeking refuge in the U.S.

Though Bernie Sanders didn't use this example during the last Democratic debate, when it came time to tighten the screws on bankruptcy laws, making it harder for poor people—often women[2]—to escape the burden of unreasonable debt, Hillary was there to do the big financial institutions' bidding[3] (the law eventually passed congress in 2005).

She has always been late to the scene, and adopts a placating rhetorical stance, on any cutting-edge progressive issue, from gay rights to drug legalization to doing something about mass incarceration, even if her policies (such as the "defense of marriage") have explicitly promoted the regressive attitudes in the first place. She likes to show up, once someone else has done the job, to pick the credit, as she did when she eagerly stood with New York governor Andrew Cuomo for passage of the $15 minimum wage, something she was opposed to in principle at the national level;[4] in any case, incrementally lifting the minimum wage to $15 in different states, in three to five to seven years, is already too little too late.

The huge affection shown for Barack Obama in the first six months of 2008 was because he came across—rather disingenuously as it turned out—as embodying feminist values. He enunciated an ethics of compassion we had sorely missed during the macho Bush years. All that

---

[1] https://www.youtube.com/watch?v=dtu50I9Imys.
[2] Marilyn Gardner, "Bankruptcy Reform Hits Women Hard," *The Christian Science Monitor*, Apr. 4, 2015: http://www.csmonitor.com/2005/0404/p13s01-wmgn.html.
[3] Bill Moyers discusses Elizabeth Warren versus Hillary Clinton on bankruptcy law: https://www.youtube.com/watch?v=4Gnu0XNPgHk.
[4] Patrick Caldwell, "Hillary Clinton Just Endorsed a $15 Minimum Wage. But Not for Everyone," *Mother Jones*, July 24, 2015.

changed as soon as his nomination was secured, and after June 2008 he had no further interest in holding anyone accountable for the vicious hypermasculine deeds of the preceding eight years.

Hillary has always undercut feminism by selectively appropriating hyperfeminine tropes when it suits her politically, undermining the ideal of the equality of men and women, including emotional equality. She calls up the tears when necessary, for example in the 2008 New Hampshire primary, to get sympathy. The entire subtext of her sixteen-year-long positioning for the presidency seems to be, I've paid my dues, especially in terms of the emotional costs, so I must have my turn. This is not a particularly empowering feminist message. Likewise, to keep repeating the one million miles she traveled and the 112 countries she visited as Secretary of State seems a throwback to the prefeminist notion of backbreaking work for its own sake. She was there, she may not have a record to point to, but she sure showed up and worked her butt off to be physically present everywhere!

I desperately wish to see a female president. It happened long ago in many other nations, some of which are not even "developed" countries by our reckoning. Sri Lanka, India, Pakistan, Bangladesh, and many others did it a while ago. Yes, it would be wonderful to have a female president, but it turns out that this time it's Bernie Sanders who comes closest to representing the feminist values of caring, trust, understanding, compassion, peace, and yes—love.

If only, for a single moment in this campaign, Hillary had showed some humanity, a momentary break from her constant triangulating and having it both ways, thinking she's obligated to always give a confusing double-edged answer to every question! She didn't do it on her 2014 book tour either, which told me she had learned nothing from the way her 2008 campaign failed to resonate with voters looking for feminist values.

She is a severely compromised candidate, because the way she articulates her policies jars so badly with what we expect of an ethics of caring. It is jarring in the same way that Condi or Carly were, and it is a particular contrast to Bernie's soft side on full display at rallies and in debates, and to Obama's softer side (at least until the summer of 2008). I don't believe the country will only accept a female president if she's dressed up in patriarchal regalia; this is yet another way Hillary has long been undermining feminism, by making us believe that actual feminist values are simply not palatable for public discourse at the national level.

Eileen Myles (a poet whom I like a lot, and who in fact wrote in praise of my first poetry book), recently wrote a defense of Hillary,[1] because "wouldn't you want...[a vagina] sitting on the chair in the Oval Office?" Indeed, Eileen, I couldn't agree more, and I respect you for your lifelong commitment to equality, but may we please get a vagina that doesn't have a patriarchal mind attached to it?

We who support Sanders are not BernieBros. Please don't demean us by calling us that. It is not about hating Hillary's gender. It is about our own desperate desire for feminist values.

---

[1] Eileen Myles, "Hillary Clinton: The Leader You Want When the World Ends," *BuzzFeed*, Feb. 23, 2016: https://www.buzzfeed.com/eileenmyles/hillary-clinton-the-leader-you-want-when-the-world-ends?utm_term=.ct8baKa4k#.seJwO6Ogj.

Hillarybots, You Blew It!
Thanks for Another Decade of War, Misery, and Scandal

> "Hillary looks so beautiful after a victory, radiant, as if she's just had a night of passionate sex with a stranger. She feeds on victory as cops do on doughnuts."
> — Facebook post by poet Nada Gordon, New York City.

New York Hillarybots are the same as Hillarybots everywhere. Only ten times worse. They were presented with a golden opportunity to stick it to the establishment that has been screwing us over for decades, making us all miserable (yes, even you New Yorkers), but they went with the cynical choice. And the majority of you voted *knowing* you were making the cynical choice.

It's not as if Sanders's was some quixotic Ralph Nader-type campaign, or he was some Green Party maverick. This was the real deal. The only way to have done this was not to start a third party, in our undemocratic system, but to take over an existing party from within. Precisely what Trump is doing. Sanders gave clear signals to progressives that he never wanted to be identified with the corrupt Democratic party establishment, and you had a problem with *that*?

Again, we're talking about the real deal. Bernie has drawn even with Hillary in national polls. Since polling began on him a year ago he has consistently done better than Hillary against every potential Republican nominee. But you, Hillarybots, went for someone who would be handily beaten by any Republican not named Trump or Cruz. You cannot argue that you made the safe electoral choice. You made the *unsafe* electoral choice, desperately wanting to preserve what your generation has already socked away, hidden from our prying eyes.

The differences between the two couldn't have been clearer. It was like Bush v. Gore all over again. Bernie even managed to arrange the debate in your own backyard, so you, New York Hillarybots, could see for yourself. In that last debate, his forthright opinions were a stark rebuke to the obfuscation Hillary offered on every issue. She wouldn't give a straight answer to a single question, as she never has in her entire political life. This is not some personality flaw. It is a clever tactic designed to accomplish in office, by incremental measures, what the right-wing ultimately wants. Make no mistake, you deliberately spurned the clear progressive choice—who offered a clarity we haven't had in my lifetime!—for the one who acts like a macho warrior in female clothing.

Some of my gay friends in New York voted for Hillary and bragged about it. Gay progressive friends voted for she who, until recently, like any old right-winger, talked about the sanctity of the man-woman relationship, the way the Methodist God himself intended it! Many of the literary people I know in New York voted for Hillary, she who doesn't have a humanist instinct in her, she who always reaches for the unimaginative concession to the dark forces rather than seeking a bold vision.

What, exactly, did you like about her, New York Hillarybots? The way she always resorts to talking about doing something "incremental"—whether it's on climate change or a living wage or college tuition or health care or mass incarceration—as a way of promoting and legitimizing precisely the kinds of policies that represent a step backward on each of these issues? You can see clearly what her trick is, you know what she's up to and which side she stands with, but you, small property-owners to the core, voted for her anyway.

You know that taking away welfare, as she and her husband did in the 1990s, was never meant to take us to some enhanced welfare system, it was just a destructive end goal, and nothing good followed it. You know that when she talks about tinkering with loans for college or tinkering with the Affordable Care Act, she is only legitimizing the privatization of services that ought to be provided for free by government in any decent democracy, as your bête noire Bernie likes to remind you.

It wasn't long ago that college was indeed more or less free. Heck, I went to college in the late eighties and early nineties, and it was mostly free then. Community college was mostly free. Great public institutions of learning were more or less free. The Ivy League gave you substantial aid, regardless of your means, so you weren't saddled with debt. We are not talking about some pie-in-the-sky scheme, we are talking about reality as it existed less than a generation ago, not to mention earlier when higher education didn't cost much in this country. And single-payer health care, as the rest of the civilized world provides it, is that too much of a stretch for you Hillarybots?

And minorities in New York, you fell for this whole shtick of Bill was the first black president, or the black community just *loves* the Clintons! These are the folks who gave you the enhanced war on drugs, harsher criminal penalties, letting loose cops in your communities with increased powers, painting one and all who's poor—black, white, or brown—as responsible for their own misery and weaning them away from expecting help from government. This Hillary, the natural antithesis of everything that should matter to you, you voted for her and rejected the guy who wants to make your life easier, give you free health care and higher education, give you a breather, for heaven's sake, it's not like he's promising to turn us overnight into Scandinavia. *Just a little breather,* for a change, you didn't even want that, Hillarybots?

Definition of a Hillarybot, *Encyclopedia of Politics*, **Entry #2,383**

A person of apparently civilized demeanor, often older than fifty, with a healthy pension fund and a decent college education, who has a nice job and either has or aspires to have grandchildren, who drives a safe Japanese vehicle, and regularly tunes into NPR to affirm liberal credentials. Unusually impervious to logic and rationality, turning every discussion, from buying a house to where to vacation, into what is *practical* and what is not. Mocks idealists, dreamers, and utopians under the age of thirty who dream of a better world. Keeps up a social media drumbeat about how anyone who says anything against her idol is a misogynist who will be called out! Justifies her idol's every sell-out by repeating the same litany of sophisms, i.e., "Hillary knows how to get things done, Hillary is practical and will work with the other side, nothing can be had for free and those who promise it are delusional, Hillary has *been there and done that,* we cannot ask for more." Sees herself (she's typically an older female) as having come by every little scrap she's earned through her own efforts alone, nobody gave her anything for free, and goshdarnit, she's not going to stand for a candidate who promises stuff for free, she's with the "realist" candidate who says we can only do a little bit more, perhaps, it's best to preserve what we've already got (with the right Supreme Court justices in place we get to keep Planned Parenthood, yay!). Keeps herself at a slight distance from the scruffier youthful types, who, to be honest, scare her a bit with all the talk of the 1% and the 99%, she was not raised to grow up in an America defined by class warfare, what's next, revolution? What happens to the grandkids in a revolution? No, it has to be a firm, steady hand at the wheel, to keep things going as they are, we're still the greatest country on earth, right? And she's a woman, for god's sake, she's had to fight for every little privilege that's come her way, she's even had to put up with that philanderer Bill for a lifetime, and this wrinkly old socialist guy from Brooklyn thinks he's going to step in, grab hold of a party he doesn't even belong to, and just take it away from her?

It makes sense that this had to happen in New York, the home of the folks who gave us the intellectual justification for the endless war on terror, for hatred and violence in perpetuity around the world, for an economic system that enslaves everyone not lucky enough to know the rules of the elite and play by them. Of course this crash to reality had to happen in the center of the American media world, the publishing world, the artistic world, the financial world. And yet you want to blame Texas and those backward Southern states for making the wrong choices?

You've already got your own, your little bit of property, your free education (of course you got it for free if you're above, say, forty or fifty), but you want to roll up the welcome mat behind you, you want to be sure no one else gets what you got. You don't say it that way, of course, you rationalize it in the language of "realism" Hillary uses, but we get it, you've done nothing less than declare war on every humane value we believe in, you are determined to have this misery outlast the rest of our lives, you're determined that all this idealism and search for honesty and feminine values ends right away, right now, just as soon as Hillary takes over and starts some new wars or escalates another round of misery at home.

But you're wrong, wrong, wrong! We will not give up so easily.

You, in the center of the world, or what passes for it, have nothing much to lose and everything to be afraid of. But what if those you think of as the masses, looking in from the outside, demand that they want some of what you have too? That's what this whole Hillary worship is about, isn't it, to stop that from happening?

To do what you have done is to acquiesce in the racism, imperialism, and classism of the Democratic party establishment, ever since it was taken over by the Clinton machine. And you went with *that*, not with the guy who told he was going to keep a distance from the stink, you went with the candidate who's right at the heart of the financial machinations to deprive everyone who is not part of the elite a fair shot at a decent life.

Thank you New York Hillarybots. Hang on to your Brooklyn brownstone and your Upper East Side digs because in the ravages of chaos and war and dislocation your macho candidate is going to engineer, you're going to have to keep close watch on every bit of what you've already got stashed away.

I promise you, we're not going away. We know that by voting for Hillary you compromised the health of planet earth by who knows what magnitude, because there is not a destructive policy she will not pursue in the name of capitalism. But in the end the small-minded ideology you represent will cease to exist, like your forerunners in either party who were enraged by the civil rights movement in the 1950s and 1960s. The next Bernie Sanders will even look young and handsome like Justin Trudeau (your worst nightmare, right?), because either the earth as we know it ends, or we move into a more humane arrangement than you Hillarybots can abide. Both cannot be true. So goodbye Paul Krugman, goodbye New York poets and writers, goodbye all of you Hillarybots who showed us your true colors and made us see where not to look for allies.

And yes, your mockery, Hillarybots, of Bush and Palin and Mitt and Trump and Cruz has no meaning at all now. *You* are the problem, you've always been the problem, you in the Democratic party who've long supported the candidates of war and misery and debt. But just think, we have gone from Ralph Nader, unable to get on the debate stage, to 30,000-person rallies in the heart of the Hillarybot establishment in New York. There will be another Bernie, there will be countless more of us, who will finish the job and take us again to America's promise.

Donald Trump Is Going to Win:
This Is Why Hillary Clinton Can't Defeat What Trump Represents

The neofascist reaction, the force behind Trump, has come about because of the extreme disembeddedness of the economy from social relations. The neoliberal economy has become *pure abstraction*; as has the market, as has the state, there is no reality to any of these things the way we have classically understood them. Americans, like people everywhere rising up against neoliberal globalization (in Britain, for example, this takes the form of Brexit, or exit from the European Union), want a return of social relations, or embeddedness, to the economy.

The Trump alliance desires to remake the world in their own image, just as the class representing neoliberal globalization has insisted on doing so. The difference couldn't be starker. Capitalism today is placeless, locationless, nameless, faceless, while Trump is talking about hauling corporations back to where they belong, in their home countries, fix them in place by means of rewards and retribution, like one handles a recalcitrant child.

Trump is a businessman, while Mitt Romney was a businessman too, yet I predict victory for the former while the latter obviously lost miserably. What is the difference? While Trump "builds" things (literal buildings), in places like Manhattan and Atlantic City, places one can recognize and identify with, and while Trump's entire life has been orchestrated around building luxury and ostentatiousness, again things one can tangibly grasp and hold on to (the Trump steaks!), Romney is the personification of a placeless corporation, making his quarter billion dollars from consulting, i.e., representing economic abstraction at its purest, serving as a high priest of the transnational capitalist class.

No one can visualize the boardroom Romney sat in, as head of Bain Capital, but, via *The Apprentice*, everyone has seen, for more than a decade, what Trump's boardroom looks like, and what it takes to be a "winner" in the real economy. What was that façade behind the collapse of fictitious corporations like Enron in the early 2000s? Trump supposedly pulled the veil off.

In the present election, Hillary Clinton represents precisely the same disembodiedness as Romney, for example because of her association with the Clinton Foundation. Where did the business of the state, while she was secretary of state, stop, and where did the business of global philanthropy (just another name for global business), begin, and who can possibly tell the difference? The maneuverings of the Clinton Foundation, in the popular imagination, are as arcane as the colossal daily transactions on the world's financial exchanges.

Everything about Clinton—and this becomes all the more marked when she takes on the (false) mantle of speaking for the underclass, with whom she bears no mental or physical resemblance—reeks of the easy mobility of the global rentier class. Their efficacy cannot be accounted for, not through the kind of democratic process that is unfolding before our eyes as a remnant of the American founding imagination, her whole sphere of movement is pure abstraction.

In this election, abstraction will clearly lose, and corporeality, even if—or particularly if—gross and vulgar and rising from the repressed, will undoubtedly win. A business tycoon who vigorously inserted himself in the imaginations of the dispossessed as the foremost exponent of birtherism surely cannot be entirely beholden to the polite elites, can he? Trump is capital, but he is not capital, he is of us but also not of us in the way that the working class desires elevation from their rootedness, still strongly identified with place and time, not outside it. After all, he posed the elemental question, *Where were you born?*

Though he is in fact the libertine (certainly not Clinton, who is libertinism's antithesis), he will be able to tar her with being permissive to an extreme degree—an "enabler," as the current jargon has it, for her husband's proclivities, for example. It has nothing to do with misogyny. It has everything to do with the kind of vocabulary that must substitute for people's real emotions, their fears and desires, in the face of an abstract market that presumes to rule out everything but the "rational" utility-maximizing motive.

For the market to exist, as classical economics would have it, there must be free buyers and sellers, competitive prices, a marketplace that remains fixed and transparent, and none of these elements exist anymore in the neoliberal economy, which seeks to stamp out the last vestiges of resistance in the most forgotten parts of the world. In fact, the market has created—in the ghost towns of the American Midwest, for example—a kind of sub-Saharan desolation, in the heartland of the country, all the better to identify the completeness of its project in the "successful" coastal cities. Trump is a messenger from the most successful of these cities, and his very jet-setting presence, in the middle of empty landscapes, provides an imaginary access point.

Darkness in the human soul is not utility-maximizing, therefore someone has to stand in for the opposite of what the market establishes as the universal solvent, and that someone, in this election, happens to be Hillary Clinton; which makes her unelectable. She will not, in fact, be able to discover, as she hasn't so far, anything like an authentic voice which can prove to the electorate that she is not that dark force the market cannot account for. But note the irony: by discrediting Clinton in this manner, the losers in the global economy are actually articulating yet another form for the decisive articulateness of the market after all!

The population across the board does not see the abstractions of the transnational capitalist class being able to solve a problem like ISIS, which represents a crisis of authority. Wasn't al-Qaeda defeated? Didn't we get Osama bin Laden's head? Then what is this lingering distaste called ISIS? Forms of darkness are easily substitutable, thus Hillary (whose synecdoche is Benghazi, or secret emails) becomes unable to speak the truth, the more she tries.

But…I do not want to claim for a minute that Trump can represent anything other than the further strengthening of neoliberal capitalism, both domestically and globally. He can only represent a further intensification, as would be true of anyone else. The total globalization of the market—our greatest of myths today, the one all-powerful entity to which all, state, civil society, and individual, have completely bent—is unstoppable. The flat earth posited by Tom Friedman in the 1990s will end up erasing all local distinctiveness, the end goal of neoliberalism. While Trump represents the desire for national regeneration—as is true of any neofascist movement—this is not possible in the twenty-first century, because the state as we have known it has ended, as has the market in the conventional understanding.

In the end, Trump cannot take charge, because *no one* can take charge. Capital today serves nothing other than capital itself. In the current post-democratic, post-"capitalism" era, the myths of regeneration propounded by Trump serve as convenient fictions, as capital well knows, and is therefore little disturbed by.

Nonetheless, Trump has brought to the surface the leftover mobs of American society, the residual unemployable, the "losers" constituting perhaps a third of society, who were never acknowledged as such during the past many cycles of political ups and downs, but who are now forcing the successful two-thirds to face up to the fictions of the market.

When Trump's masses see Clinton tacking to the middle—as she undoubtedly will, rather than go for the surefire path to victory by heading left, by picking Bernie Sanders for example—the more they will detest it, which will push her only further in their direction, not in the direction that can bring victory. Clinton, because of her disembodied identity in the placeless global economy, cannot make a movement toward the direction of reality, because the equations would falter, the math would be off, the logic would be unsustainable. And that is the contradiction that the country can easily see, that is the exposed front of the abstract market that will bring about its supposed reckoning in the form of Clinton's defeat.

But the reckoning, again, will be pure fiction. Trump is not a fascist father figure, he is not the second coming of Mussolini, he is the new virtual figure who is as real as reality television, which is even more recessive and vanishing compared to Ronald Reagan's Hollywood fictions. The field of action in which Trump specialized for a long time before the nation, as dress rehearsal for the current (and final) role, was one where, at least to outward appearances, the presence of surplus capital was acknowledged and taken for granted, and aspirants competed to know more about it and to desperately work on its behalf.

With the ascension of Trump, an entire country of apprentices wants to get a handle on surplus capital by bringing the state back in, but as I said before, this is impossible because the pre-neoliberal state is gone, it has been reduced to the market, it *is* the market. Again, capital serves only capital, though Trump's followers wish to see him create a split whereby they can enter the picture, forcibly, though even they perhaps know that Trump, as president, cannot sue evanescent corporations, or other realities of the market, even if suing is a tendency that comes naturally to him.

To take the logic one step further, the myth of the market—or the way "government" is run today—cannot acknowledge one thing and one thing only: death. If you compete (whether in Trump's boardroom or on the "level playing field" he wants to bring about in America by excluding illegal competitors, whether undocumented aliens or Chinese currency manipulators or unwanted Mexican goods), you win. (Of course, this only strengthens the myth of the market, but that is something that will be evident to the populace once Trump is in power; they want a localized, responsive, non-idle market, but the market is beyond the need to accommodate itself in those ways.)

But to get back to death, Trump's campaign has been successful so far, and will surely be victorious in the end, because he is the only one who has brought death back into the discourse.

The only people identified with death today on the global scene—the only people not part of the market and not able to be part of it—are terrorists, undocumented immigrants, the homeless and the mentally ill, those who have no claims to success in the market. Trump's people want to make sure—from the purest feeling of shame known to politics—that they are not of the unchosen ones, they want to enforce a radical separation between their kind of shame, which they think is unwarranted, by excluding illegal competition, by constructing literal walls to keep out the death-dealers, by overruling the transnational party elites who have sold them out.

Trump is vocally identifying the death aura, prodding the working class to confront the other, which is as alienated and excluded as itself, but which the working class likes to imagine is the irreconcilable other. By forcing this confrontation he has put himself in the winner's seat.

Let us note the rise of suicide among white working-class men and women, of all ages. This—like the other deals in death that the market fails to name—is an assertion of independence from the market.

Let us note too the power of the transgender rights movement (after the relative normalization of the presence of AIDS, and also of same-sex marriage) to prompt ferocious emotions amongst the excluded; this movement has become a substitute for the power of death—sexual death—to terrify us. They would rather be terrified by something they can do something about, knowing that the market wants to assimilate this form of gender-bending, identity-shifting, unlocalizable personality triumph. Again, Trump is virtual but not virtual, he is of TV but not of TV, functioning more as an ambassador from TV than an actor or role-player in that world—which makes him uniquely equipped, in the eyes of his supporters, for taking on the kinds of death-dealers that they think mess up the market against their parochial interests.

Think again of Trump's initiation of his campaign with the idea of *the wall*, and calling those who break through the wall rapists and murderers.

And compare it to Clinton's opening gambit of giving identifiable personalities to the clear winners in the transnational race to acquire and embody capital, paraded one after the other in her first campaign commercial. And then think of the culture warriors, both on the left and the right, as perceiving every threat as a personal attack on their very being, their very existence, no matter how trivial the offence (hence the revealing term "*micro*-aggressions), exactly as the Trump proletariat reacts to attacks on their identity, as they have been trained to respond after decades of rampant identity politics. Now consider, in the face of these three competing tendencies, the market's pure victory; because all three games are being played out on its terms, it is the preordained winner. And yet, I would say, Trump must win, he has to win, to give the element he represents, of the three mentioned here, a degree of equality with the other two. The spectacle must be kept interesting after all.

What is common between the "multitudes" who show up for the Trump and Sanders rallies? Both constituencies are rebelling against the empire of capital, the empire of the market (whether the right calls it the New World Order or the left calls it free trade), and they show up naming empire as such. In this election campaign, whoever *names* the empire of the market wins (Trump, or Sanders had he been able to overcome the barriers erected by the Democratic party), and whoever hides its name (Clinton), loses. Are these rallies, Trump's and Sanders's, aesthetic spectacles, or are they radical politics? The market does not have an answer to this question, or rather it has already answered it to its own satisfaction.

Is Trump a racist? Does he represent racists? We have to take into account the fact that the recent resurgence of racism—in the form of overt police beatings, for example, and other things that we thought had been relegated to the past—is a symptom of the failure of the old state, it is simply an assertion on the part of the market that we cannot count on the "state" as such to resolve the fantasy of racism as the great equalizer. The market, I would dare to assert, is quite happy at the failure of the state to contend with racism. And to the extent that Trump fans the flames of racism, the market is happy with that too, it remains above the fray, so to speak, it remains the only untouched, unsullied, uncorrupted entity in the whole ongoing show.

I expect Trump to take a national lead shortly and never relinquish it until the end. It will be easy if he keeps the libertine and destructive aspects of himself in perfect balance, seesawing from one to the other, as he has so far, appealing to an elemental fear in the country, torn apart by the abstraction of the market, to which Clinton has not the faintest hope of responding. He only has to use one distinctively non-misogynist, concretely unifying, morose five-letter word in the debates: NAFTA. A pure market abstraction that has turned out to be not so much an abstraction.

The Millennial Generation Is a Perfect Fit for Socialism

Few developments have caused as much consternation amongst advocates of "free-market capitalism" recently as various findings that millennials, compared to previous generations, are exceptionally receptive to socialism.

A recent Reason-Rupe survey[1] found that a majority of Americans under thirty have a more favorable view of socialism than of capitalism. Gallup finds that almost seventy percent of young Americans[2] are ready to vote for a "socialist" president. So it has come as no surprise that seventy to eighty percent of young Americans have been voting for Bernie Sanders,[3] the self-declared democratic socialist.

Pundits have been eager to denounce[4] such surveys as momentary aberrations, stemming from the economic crash, or due to lack of knowledge on the part of millennials about the authoritarianism they say is the inevitable result of socialism. They were too young to have been around for Stalin and Mao, they didn't experience the cold war, they don't know to be grateful to capitalism for saving them from global tyranny. The critics dismiss the millennials' political leanings by repeating Margaret Thatcher and Ronald Reagan's mantra, which prompted the

---

[1] Emily Ekins, "Poll: Americans Like Free Market More Than Capitalism and Socialism More Than a Govt. Managed Economy," *Reason*, Feb. 12, 2015: http://reason.com/poll/2015/02/12/poll-americans-like-free-markets-more-th.
[2] http://www.gallup.com/poll/183713/socialist-presidential-candidates-least-appealing.aspx.
[3] Aaron Blake, "74-Year-Old Bernie Sanders's Remarkable Dominance Among Young Voters, in One Chart," *Washington Post*, March 17, 2016: https://www.washingtonpost.com/news/the-fix/wp/2016/03/17/74-year-old-bernie-sanderss-amazing-dominance-among-young-voters-in-1-chart/?utm_term=.588ed942fc46.
[4] Jonah Goldberg, "Millennials Embrace Socialism, But Do They Know What It is?" *National Review*, May 13, 2016: http://www.nationalreview.com/article/435326/bernie-sanders-millennials-socialism-what-exactly.

extreme form of capitalism we now know as neoliberalism, that "There is No Alternative" (TINA).

But millennials, in the most positive turn of events since the economic collapse, intuitively understand better. Circumstances not of their choosing have forced them to think outside the capitalist paradigm, which reduces human beings to figures of sales and productivity, and to consider if in their immediate lives, and in the organization of larger collectivities, there might not be more cooperative, nonviolent, mutually beneficial arrangements with better measures of human happiness than GDP growth or other statistics that benefit the financial class.

Indeed, the criticism most heard against the millennial generation's evolving attachment to socialism is that they don't understand what the term really means, indulging instead in warm fuzzy talk about *cooperation* and *happiness*. But this is precisely the larger meaning of socialism, which the millennial generation—as evidenced in the Occupy and Black Lives Matter movements—totally comprehends.

Capitalism has only itself to blame, forcing millennials to look for an alternative.

Let's recall a bit of recent history before amnesia completely erases it. While banks were bailed out to the tune of trillions of dollars (the actual commitment of the U.S. government was $16 trillion to corporations and banks worldwide, as revealed in a 2011 audit prompted by Senator Sanders and others),[1] the government was not interested in offering serious help to individuals carrying underwater mortgages. Facing crushing amounts of debt, millennials have been forced to cohabit with their parents and to downshift ambitions. They have had to relearn the habits of communal living, making do with less, and they are bartering necessary skills because of the permanent casualization of jobs. They are questioning the value of a capitalist education that prepares them for an ideology that is vanishing and an economy that doesn't exist.

After the Great Depression, regulated capitalism did a good enough job keeping people's ideas of happiness in balance. Because of job stability, wage growth, and opportunities for mobility, primarily driven by progressive taxation and generous government services, regulated capitalism experienced its heyday during 1945-1973, not just in America but around the world. Since then, however, the Keynesian insight that a certain level of equality must be maintained to preserve capitalism has

---
[1] http://www.sanders.senate.gov/newsroom/press-releases/the-fed-audit.

been abandoned in favor of a neoliberal regime that has privatized, deregulated, and "liberalized" to the point where extreme inequality, a new form of serfdom, has come into being.

Millennials perceive that what is on offer in this election cycle on the part of one side (Trump) is a return to a regulated form of capitalism, but with a frightening nationalist overlay and a disregard for the environment that is not sustainable, and on the other side (Clinton) a continuation of the neoliberal ideology of relying exclusively on the market to make the best decisions on behalf of human welfare. They understand that the "reforms" of the last eight years have been so mild, as with the Dodd-Frank bill, as to keep neoliberalism in its previous form intact, guaranteeing future cycles of debt, insolvency, and immiseration. They haven't forgotten that the capitalist class embarked on an *austerity* campaign, of all things, in 2009 in the U.S. and Europe, precisely the opposite of what was needed to alleviate misery.

But millennials are done with blind faith in the market as the solution to all human problems. They question whether "economic growth" should even be the ultimate pursuit. Ironically, again, it is the extreme form capitalism has taken under neoliberalism that has put millennials under such pressure that they have started asking these questions seriously: Why not work fewer hours? Why not disengage from consumer capitalism? Why trust in capitalist goods to buy happiness? Why not discover the virtues of community, solidarity, and togetherness? It is inchoate still, but this sea change in the way a whole generation defines *happiness* is what is going to determine the future of American politics.

Millennials understand that overturning capitalist memes to address the immediate social and ecological crises is only the starting point. The more difficult evolution is to reorient human thought, after more than five hundred years of capitalist hegemony, to think beyond even democratic or participatory socialism, to a more anarchic, more liberated social organization, where individuals have the potential to achieve freedom and self-realization, precisely the failed promise of capitalism.

To distract attention by pointing to the failure of authoritarian state-driven experiments in socialism is not going to work. Cooperative models not driven by the state have been pervasive throughout history, all through the middle ages for example, or until recently in large parts of the world where capitalism hadn't yet penetrated. Whenever one forms a spontaneous association to fulfill real needs, whether in a family or community or town, one is embarking on activity that is discounted by capitalism.

In the nineteenth century, there was the successful cooperative model of Robert Owen, the British cotton-spinner and industrialist, followed in the twentieth century with similar ventures by Owen's counterpart in Japan, Muto Sanji, as well as agricultural, industrial, housing, and banking cooperatives in Australia in the early twentieth century, in the Basque region of Spain after the second world war, in Italy's Emilia-Romagna, and in Sweden, Canada, Denmark, and elsewhere. Today, many examples of the cooperative model operate in Brazil,[1] Venezuela,[2] and other Latin American countries, spurred by resistance to the neoliberal model.

The idea is to move beyond money,[3] interpreted in particular ways by capitalism, as the sole means of determining what is valued in human activity. Just because the means of production can be owned collectively does not mean—and indeed should not mean—that the *state* should be the owner.

In effect, capitalism is losing its future constituency, not just in America, but in other parts of the world as well. It happened among millennials in Latin America in the last decade, as indigenous movements sprouted up, avowing to chart a non-authoritarian path compared to socialisms of the past, all this as the clash between capitalism's totalizing logic and the health of the planet reached a crescendo.

The current American election is one of the last of the rearguard actions by so-called progressives exploiting the notion that nothing better is possible. This anti-humanism, masquerading as pragmatism, asks millennials to buy into the idea that we can only expect the false measures of happiness that capitalism has sold us on.

Cooperation is neither medieval nor tyrannizing; it is rather avant-garde, and it looks like the millennial generation is ready to ride the wave. Millennials are famously optimistic; socialism was designed for just such a breed.

---

[1] Carl Ratner, "Cooperative Economics in Brazil: The UNISOL Economic Network," Grassroots Economic Organizing (GEO), 2015.
[2] Michael Snow, "Cooperation, Co-operatives, and Revolution in Venezuela," Venezuela Analysis, June 22, 2012: https://venezuelanalysis.com/analysis/7067.
[3] http://cultivate.coop/wiki/Worker_Cooperatives.

Thank you, Donald Trump:
The Left Ignores the Intellectual Substance of Trumpism at its Own Peril

As the mainstream media keep up their relentless barrage of violent criticism of Donald Trump's personal foibles, and as Hillary Clinton's campaign takes advantage of it in a manner that seems clearly coordinated, the genuine concerns of nearly half of all Americans Donald Trump has tapped into are being ignored and sidelined by the intellectual elite. But Trumpism is a new constitution of populist authoritarianism in America, a permanent ideological tendency that will not fade away regardless of the outcome of this election.

In one sense—having been up against the entire political and intellectual establishment—Trump has already come out the winner, because he has put into radical doubt (as did Bernie Sanders on the other side) the neoliberal consensus around which both major parties and their institutional supporters cohere in Washington. His is a renegade candidacy that will have a lasting impact on world politics, though it is easy to overlook this amidst the din of moral righteousness currently trumped up by the establishment.

Whether or not Trump is a neo-fascist is less interesting than tracing his similarities to European right-wing populists like Jean-Marie Le Pen, Jörg Haider, Umberto Bossi, Gianfranco Fini, and others. It can't be denied that every extreme right-wing movement has a tendency to slip into overt fascism at times, as when entire populations are targeted for exclusion and punishment. But to understand Trumpism we are better off searching for familiar strains in American populism, from Father Coughlin to George Wallace, from Huey Long to Pat Buchanan. I mention Long, the populist governor of Louisiana during the Great Depression, because there are elements of Trump's critique that have something of the redistributive element as well, though Coughlin's charismatic media presence, Wallace's appeal to white supremacy, and

Buchanan's America First xenophobia and protectionism are clearer markers of Trumpism's homegrown origins.

Because Trump has taken his blunt critique of elite politics farther than any of his recent predecessors in the major parties, sometimes it appears that he is manifesting Mussolini-like fascist tendencies, but to think like this would be to stretch fascism's definition beyond meaningfulness. Fascism is the close alliance of corporations and government in a movement of national regeneration, mobilizing the resentful parts of the population toward racist and militarist aims. Though Trump likes to say that he's fond of the military, I do not see war as being a priority for him; nor do I see the integral corporate-government merger that is a sine qua non of fascism; and nor do Trumpists seem to have any enthusiasm to dissolve their personal identities in the cause of the state, as is true of fascism.

The closest we came to fascism was in the 2001-2003 Bush period, as I often noted at the time, but at that point hardly anyone in the commentariat was interested in picking up that frame of reference; now they throw the term around whenever someone utters anything the least bit racist or xenophobic. The deployment of the epithet becomes hollow and dismissive. Indeed, it was said about Italian fascism that it had no ideological content, which excused European liberals in the 1920s and 1930s from addressing the root causes of the movement and allowed them the kind of moral distancing that we see again in the American intellectual reaction toward Trumpism.

Trump does, however, have the charisma that Bush the younger lacked, which, among other reasons, makes me convinced that November 8 will not be the end of his movement. I have believed for many years that about a third of the population is primed to a message of his kind at any given time, but this proportion can go up to fifty percent or more during crises. There is no way that the Republican party will be able to reassemble the coalition that has defined it since the Reagan years. Trump has questioned the fetish for "small government" in substantive ways, sidelined evangelical Christians for the first time in thirty-five years (though he makes a feint at acceding to their sensitivities), and blown the cover on the bipartisan neoliberal consensus around trade, taxes, immigration, and other economic issues. Whatever happens on election day, there will be a new reckoning for Republicans—and for Democrats as well.

It is indeed helpful to look at the precedents of the various right-wing populist movements in Europe over the last four decades to understand Trumpism. Every major European country has had its parallel movement, which arose in reaction to a new form of globalization (or postindustrial modernization) that began eroding the security of middle-class constituencies, and which targeted some typical scapegoats to alleviate their anxieties: foreign workers, refugees and asylum seekers, and Muslims, above all.

The Front National (FN) in France, the Freedom Party (FPÖ) in Austria, the Lega Nord and Alleanza Nationale (AN) in Italy, the Vlaams Block (VB) in Belgium, the Progress parties in Denmark and Norway and the New Democracy party in Sweden, the NPD, DVU, and REP in Germany, the Center Party and Center Democrats in the Netherlands, the Democratic Union of the Center (DUC) in Switzerland, the British National Party (BNP) in Britain, and the Reform Party in Canada, to mention some of the prominent examples, are all direct precursors of Trumpism, bearing strong similarities across time and space, patterns of resentment and mobilization that Trump is faithfully replicating in his movement.

All of these parties are populist in the sense that they refuse the elite consensus around the contours of governance amidst postindustrial transformation, and they refuse, as well, the accompanying and essential cultural consensus, namely multiculturalism, that all Western democracies have adopted in some form or another to go along with the neoliberal economic creed. One does not find, in any of these parties, a purely economic critique centered around trade and protectionism, or welfare and taxes; rather there is always a corresponding cultural counterinsurgency as well, namely around breaking the various taboos and silences that have been imposed by the neoliberal elite on what is or is not acceptable social behavior in the new economic milieu.

So contemporary neo-populism is better understood not in terms of the earlier fascist model, but as a productivist impulse that identifies collectivist groups supposedly benefiting from multiculturalism as standing in the way of entrepreneurial individualism. To some extent, indeed, there is truth to the alleged chain of causation, since it is the offshoring of manufacturing to cheaper Asian locations that has caused the erosion of the manufacturing base in the Western democracies, and likewise it is the exploitative importation of cheap labor that helps create a downward push on wages for native white populations.

Of course, to stop at this point in the analysis—as unfortunately neo-populists do—is to grievously abridge the logic of economic inequality, which, if it is to be complete, must take in the overall composition of neoliberal economic philosophy. In fact, to a large extent, the productivist mentality enshrined in Trumpism and European populist authoritarianism is as much a reflection of neoliberalist individualism as it is a yearning for the principles of nineteenth-century laissez-faire economics.

Trumpism and allied movements cannot take on globalization without also taking on multiculturalism. The neo-populists see no way around neoliberal globalization except through overcoming multiculturalism. They see those unfairly benefiting from the multicultural model as being the cause of their misery, their perpetual uncertainty in the new economy, because there is no telling when their jobs might be permanently lost due to lower wages in other countries or because of unfair competition from immigrants who ought to have less of a rightful claim than natives. Whether it's called France for the French, Germany for the Germans, or Make America Great Again, the idea is the same.

The Brexiteers knew well that they wanted to blow up the system which wasn't working for them; every charge by the American media that Trump wants to do the same only makes him more popular among his supporters, since that is exactly what they want. That's the level of deprivation a quarter-century of unresponsiveness by the governing elites has brought them to.

The language of multiculturalism that comes so smoothly to elites on either side of the Atlantic is *precisely* the problem for neo-populists. End the reproduction of this language and you end the transmission of new mechanisms of globalized production and exchange, they tend to believe. Trump, in this country, has made this connection more explicit, more robust, and more durable than anyone in the past. He speaks a constantly irritating politically incorrect speech because it is central to his critique that the decks are stacked against hardworking Americans—real Americans, white Americans—who cannot get ahead despite their best efforts because there is a conspiracy of intolerance against their individualist mores (here, guns and the Second Amendment come in as crucial elements of the mythology of victimhood, as well as explicit refutation of the politically correct language that has developed around race, religion, and gender).

There has been much speculation about the class basis of Trump's support, as the elite media, often without much data, concludes that the average Trump supporter tends to be better off than the average Clinton or Sanders supporter. This conveniently ignores the huge numbers of unemployed or underemployed Americans, those on the economic margins who do not see a way back in, who manifestly appear at Trump rallies around the country. This also allows the establishment media to dismiss Trumpism as a hissy fit, a momentary aberration amongst relatively advantaged people (for one thing because they are white!) that will be over just as soon as the election is done.

The key point that is missed is that Trumpists view themselves as beset by anxieties, whether or not their actual economic standing reflects the heightened state of their worry and resentment. Some of them may be definitionally middle-class, but they do not see themselves as functionally middle-class, and certainly not emotionally middle-class. As Trump resonantly declared, addressing these people in the most rhetorically persuasive convention speech I have witnessed, "I am your voice."

I have always viewed multiculturalism as neoliberalism's ideological arm, a methodology for neoliberalism, for the last twenty-five years, to divorce culture from economics, movements of individual liberation from class consciousness, offering a form of recognition that rests on isolation, fragmentation, and segregation, rather than universal human values. Thankfully, Trumpists also see multiculturalism the same way, a technique the neoliberal elites have adopted to present themselves as self-righteous moralists while doing nothing about the economic causes of their misery. They have seen through the act.

History shows that the support base for right-wing extremist movements tends to be primarily the petty bourgeoisie—small businesspeople, professionals at the lower levels—but populism never gets far without the support of large numbers of the permanently unemployed. The official economic statistics would have us believe—and Trump vigorously contests this—that we are at or near full employment. In fact, this is a gross deception, because there are tens of millions of Americans who have given up looking for employment, who for various reasons are not employable in any meaningful sense of the word. Trump claims it is thirty percent of the population, but whatever number it really is, experience shows that it is pervasive, outside a few humming urban centers that give the illusion of high employment. As a matter of policy, the U.S. has not been committed to full employment since the 1970s, as part of the anti-inflationary monetary policy inaugurated by Paul Volcker and carried on by other committed neoliberals.

It is interesting to read bemused articles by correspondents at elite magazines like the *Atlantic* and the *New Yorker*, wondering about who the Trump supporters really are (as they do after every populist upsurge), acting as though they were writing about aliens from another planet (which they are in a sense, the elite commentators being unable to understand why the Trumpists take such a dire view of the economy, since everything, from their point of view, seems pretty decent, with a 5% unemployment rate, the stock market doing well, and the evidence of their own booming urban areas).

Trump is not incorrect when he paints his picture of hell in American cities. I am fortunate to live in Montrose, the bohemian but rapidly gentrifying part of Houston, Texas, and while the small cultural district is livable, even pleasant, enormous swaths of the larger Houston metropolitan area seem to have been abandoned to a primal wilderness, lacking basic infrastructure, decent schools, safety and recreation, even access to good food and clean air and water. Directly east of downtown lies the Fifth Ward, as close a realization of Trump's apocalyptic vision as I have ever seen. But it is not just the Fifth Ward, it is vast territories that have been left to wither and die, as neoliberal municipal governments commit their resources to recreating central city zones as arenas for spectacular multiculturalism (which translates into gigantic bounties for real estate developers), while withdrawing financial support for neighborhoods outside the elite zones.[1]

In the absence of any effort by the neoliberal elites to provide an explanation for historically high levels of permanent unemployment, both in Western Europe and the United States, right-wing populism leeches on to the idea of unfair labor market penetration into heritage occupations, unfair trade agreements benefiting countries on the economic periphery, and unfair racial policies and preference quotas advantaging those without qualifications. This is not a rational way of thinking, but it is a self-consistent logic, which becomes all the more hardened the more the elite neoliberals deny the very existence of such concerns. It is in the latter's interest to promote trade and immigration

---
[1] I discussed the adverse impact of gentrification in Houston here:
http://www.salon.com/2014/11/28/how_oligarchs_destroyed_a_major_american_city_partner/.

along strictly neoliberal lines, benefiting the capitalist class at the very top and leaving everyone else worse off.

Some seem to look at the forty percent support Trump always seems to settle around as his ceiling, but I choose to look at it as his floor, a level of adherence that isn't likely to go away in the new Republican party that we are going to see constituted in the wake of the election. The degree of support for Trumpism has become constant because the Democratic party has forced down our throats not the clear popular choice for the nominee, i.e., Bernie Sanders, but the candidate that was at the absolute forefront of the accelerated second phase of neoliberalism during the Bill Clinton presidency (after the relatively tentative and half-successful stabs at it in the Reagan era).

We could have had a clear choice, dictated by democratic forces, between democratic socialism (Bernie Sanders) and populist authoritarianism (Donald Trump), a contest that would have been bracingly clarifying, a turning point that would have brought into being new alignments, new political realities. What we got instead—because of Democratic party shenanigans, the entire party establishment conspiring with Hillary Clinton and her brand of neoliberalism, from Jerry Brown in California to Sherrod Brown in Ohio, buttressed by the liberal apparatus from the media to the academy—is a contest between the old neoliberalism and an amped-up right-wing populism, except that in this case, because of media demonization of Trump, neoliberalism has received a free pass during this election cycle from explaining any policy outcomes.

We might even say that what we're actually getting now is not a contest between neoliberalism and Trumpism, but that because the media has written Trump out of the equation altogether in the latter stages of this campaign, we are now hearing neoliberalism fight it out with its supercharged ideal, which would be Hillary if she were a perfect multiculturalist, without any of her baggage.

But I am certain that the inevitable reckoning has only been deferred. The neoliberal elites, soon after the electoral rituals are over, will desperately try to change the subject with the instigation of crisis, mostly likely war (as they did in the wake of the antiglobalization protests of the late 1990s). But Trump has consolidated right-wing populism to a more defined extent than anything previously seen in modern American politics, he has solidified a base which is not going to relinquish prominence under any circumstances, and which, in fact, should propel the corresponding rise of a democratic socialist movement on the left, whether or not it is under Sanders's direction.

Imagine if Trump had faced off Clinton in the primaries. Think of how easily he disposed of "low-energy" Jeb Bush (the Republican version of Hillary) by assailing his brother for letting 9/11 happen on his watch and for his failed Iraq War, breaking sacrosanct Republican taboos. Whenever in this campaign the media has taken a break from scandals, and Trump has been allowed to focus on ideas, he has made gains in electoral standing. This was true during August above all as he focused on his signature economic ideas, and this would have been very true after the second debate, when he finally took on Clinton's corruption head-on and stayed on his economic message, had it not been for the media's self-righteous focus on his politically incorrect persona, the one surefire way to bypass and invalidate any underlying causes of the malaise his supporters (the "basket of deplorables") feel. Once Donald Trump has been made to morph into Bill Cosby, we need not take him seriously; he is dehumanized, as are his supporters.

After all, Hillary Clinton cannot possibly engage in a substantive discussion with Trump. It's unfortunate that he lacks the intellectual acumen to probe each problem to its origin, and he is also restrained from pursuing obvious lines of inquiry because of his own right-wing ideology, but how could the politician who, during the 1990s, most typified everything that is essential of neoliberalism, who threw her weight behind every important move in that direction, possibly defend the outcomes? She vigorously supported NAFTA and other trade agreements, welfare reform, crime and terrorism initiatives, punitive measures against immigrants that halted the liberalization in place since the 1965 immigration act, the downsizing of government, the inflation of housing and other bubbles, and the deregulation of banking, telecommunications, and other industries with dire consequences in the following decade.

Trump was right during the debates when he pointed out her legacy of inaction toward causes she now wants to champion, and he was right to mock her for directing people to the policies inscribed on her website; I have visited there too, and I fail to see the slew of statements as anything other than campaign fodder, rhetorical devices that do not exist at any realistic level, since nothing there has any chance of coming to fruition in the absence of control of both houses of congress; and even if the House were to be captured by some miracle, there would not be a move to realize anything like the true progressive policies—free college, universal healthcare, a just wage, and an end to wars—that constituted Sanders's agenda.

What you see on Hillary's website are theoretical insinuations to recoup some minute incrementals of the New Deal consensus that she herself was instrumental, above anyone else besides her husband, in shattering and destroying during the 1990s. So the very person who brought about the neoliberal corporate state—a fundamental shift that occurred in the early 1990s, making us a different kind of country than even what we had known in the Reagan years—now promises to regain a tiny fraction of it, not by pursuing the universal welfare policies of the New Deal, but what we might call fatalist incrementalism or pessimistic consensualism. And that's at the rhetorical level, before any negotiations take place with a hard-boiled anti-welfare ideologue like Paul Ryan.

While Democrats act self-righteously about Trump's rhetoric toward immigrants, let us note that immigration as a contemporary problem first truly manifested itself during the Clinton administration, with the onset of NAFTA, the immiseration of parts of Mexico which led to a surge of new forms of migration, the technical barriers that were erected to make legalization less possible than in earlier years, the huge backlogs that emerged in the process of resistance to administrative discretion that used to be the norm, and the onset of demonization of immigrants (as potential terrorists, criminals, and abusers of the welfare system) that had not been seen since the Great Depression. Reagan and the elder Bush were the last two presidents to hold a humanitarian immigration outlook.

Trump may talk of a Muslim ban, but Clintonian neoliberalism created an enormous immigration problem, preventing normal legalization, a legacy that Bush and Obama confronted with unprecedented levels of deportation. Immigrants have became a tool that the neoliberal elite continues to exploit to the full in their transformation of the American economy, depriving them of their legitimate rights as a way to drive down wages for all and to mount a broad-based assault on civil liberties for all. We are bearing the fruits of those years now. Not once have I ever heard the Clintons or Obama make a comprehensive moral—or even economic—case for immigration; when you are enforcement-only and not idealists or humanitarians, then soon an even greater enforcer will come and take your place.

Likewise, when it comes to Trump's issues with women, let us note the transcendent dimension of it, of which Hillary Clinton is a major culprit, along with academics and politicians who, during the 1990s, created structures of mental classification and separation that remain divisive to this day. Just as an example, to engineer "welfare reform," retreating from a core moral commitment of the New Deal, the black woman of political mythology who was supposedly the prime recipient of such aid had to be demonized as a nonproductive citizen, her body and environment and heritage had to be problematized as worthy of correction by managerial means, in order that she might overcome "dependency" and derive the moral benefits of employment.

Needless to say, that experiment has been a failure, as entire populations have been abandoned to poverty, or at best low-wage employment that interferes with the care of children and families. This is not to mention incalculable numbers of other peoples affected by the neoliberal policies of systematic exploitation and cultural and aesthetic genocide. There are levels of exploitation and degradation; Trump's has been distinctly minor league, he has hardly had recourse to the flourishing arsenals of power that a politician like Hillary Clinton has thrived on. The underlying case for welfare reform was built on depicting welfare-receiving women as fat, lazy, sleazy, and promiscuous, an actionable universal category, compared to the contemporary phenomenon of body-shaming by Trump as a purely personal construct in an entertainment context.

We have to go back to the problem of insecurity created amongst the tentative middle-class, Trump's base of supporters, a direct result of the revolutionary reengineering of American governance during the Clinton era. The compact between government and citizens was broken in those years, and was replaced by nothing new, a vacuum that Trumpism is stepping into now, especially because the corrupt Democratic party ensured that Sanders's left populism wasn't legitimized.

To further shift the focus from Trump's alleged immoral supporters to the systematic immorality that is neoliberalism, I would like to offer these speculations:

1. Trumpism is creating a new form of cultural capital, distorted and perverted though it may be, as is true of all right-wing populism or neo-fascism. The academic left has held a monopoly for a long time on self-righteousness, which has lately, in the present form of political correctness, burst forth in a relentless pseudo-self-criticism amongst intellectuals, aiming to purge the protagonists of their own white guilt.

Trumpism forms a counter to this elite self-flagellation by offering an empowered version of popular white supremacy, to not only oppose the imposition of guilt but reorient the polity toward productivist rather than nonproductivist explanations of economic decline.

In other words, shame has been lent an economic, not a cultural, veneer, in the new movement. This is a massive breakthrough, just as Ralph Nader, and then Bernie Sanders, also sought to disconnect cultural rhetoric from economic causes. Trumpism may, quite possibly, emerge in the long run as a bridge—an unsteady one, for the moment, no doubt—to a postcapitalist libertarianism, even a left anarchism, which seems inevitable as the twenty-first century goes along.

2. Sanders's message was so popular amongst millennials because he identified a few core solutions to economic inequality, relentlessly hammered at them (just as Trump does in a distorted manner from the other side of the political spectrum), rather than rehearse multicultural pieties. I believe that the collective Trumpian cultural capital is now stabilized, regardless of the outcome of the election, and ready to emerge from the fringes of the media spectrum.

Can we also say that Sanders's movement was a left-libertarianism that dared to exclude the moral impositions of academic multiculturalism? And if that's the case, then can Trumpism, in future iterations, also move in a parallel libertarian direction? It seems to me that neither Trump nor Sanders's nascent movements can be absorbed and assimilated in either major party as presently constituted, so we must look to some fundamental change as neoliberalism encounters further domestic and foreign failures (probably in the Middle East, soon to be the next president's playground).

3. Trumpism turns the logic of multiculturalism, i.e., difference, to a new form of segregation. The European neo-populist parties all exploit the fear of the immigrant in three different dimensions—economic, cultural, and moral—amounting to defense of the race, purification of the body politic, and expulsion of the polluting and criminal and irredeemably alien. Extremist populism is inherent in multiculturalism's ultimate logic, because Trumpism is simply "diversity" carried to the national level; as with the Brexiteers, Trumpists posit the right of America to be different, morally eccentric and ornery and noncompliant,

rather than accept the loss of national identity amidst the cold conquest of markets and territories.

It is a turning inward that can have rich psychological rewards for protagonists overcome by economic anxiety. Trumpism has created the equation, economic protectionism = cultural protectionism, in common with its European forerunners. We may say that in its extreme form, Trumpism is an attempted return to *precapitalism*, moving back toward uncertainties in trade and rejecting the compulsions of empire that yield certainties (hence the skepticism toward NATO and nuclear non-proliferation regimes and other establishment verities).

I will end by saying that it is also possible to read Trumpism in an entirely different way, which would still be self-consistent: *as a pure form of neoliberalism*, supplemented by a racist or differential veneer, or we might say minus the multicultural distraction that interferes with social darwinist logic proceeding to its final conclusion, exterminating the weak other, the vulnerable environment, all species and beings not conducive to financial success.

We might then interpret the 2000s as a passing phase of neoliberalism, when it was militarist and outwardly directed, not at all given to rumination, but now entering a premodern xenophobic phase, all the easier to blanket the planet with a commercializing logic that will withstand no criticism. In this perspective, Hillary's incremental fatalism (or what passes as such for popular consumption), her commitment to neoliberal identity claims (one group after another marginally recognized at a time), is perhaps one of the final manifestations of a failed sociability.

Though Bernie's articulation was the right one for this time and place, there is a lot that Trump, in a distorted, weird way, got right about our situation:

* Both parties are corrupt and beholden to the same oligarchic interests, and Trump had the audacity to point it out, eliciting, I'm sure, exclamations of relief and pleasure at the piercing of the protective veneer neoliberal chieftains like Hillary Clinton have constructed around themselves. He asked for her to be put in jail for the wrong reasons at the second debate, but the neoliberal gerarchy's innumerable crimes against humanity, from illegal wars to the mistreatment of prisoners, deserve nothing less.

* By focusing on a stark financial calculus (we will all be "winners" in the Trumpian economy, or at least white Americans, the right Americans, will be), he has blown up the dominance of evangelical Christianity on the right side of the spectrum, as far as I can tell.

* He has exposed, by inscribing it in action and speech, the hypocrisies of the academic multiculturalists, who to the Trumpists, not to mention libertarians, embody a self-censoring authoritarian language that does not allow rational thinking to take place.

* He has pointed out the true extent of unemployment (it is said of the European neo-populists that they arose in the face of permanent unemployment, a phenomenon French and German thinkers call "civilisation du chômage," or civilization of unemployment), which mars, above all, the African-American and Hispanic zones of habitation in America's cities, landscapes of apocalyptic misery that have received no recognition from the neoliberal masters; he has a point when he asks African Americans, "What do you have to lose?"

* He is a crude simplifier, but he has described, from the other side of the political spectrum than Sanders, intractable problems with the neoliberal conceptions of trade, modernity, and empire. He seems far less interested than Hillary Clinton, for example, in starting a confrontation with Russia in the Middle East.

Once upon a time the Clintons took over a Democratic party, insecure about its electoral prospects at the national level, and converted it from the inside into something it never was before: a party of neoliberal elitists, beholden to a new moral righteousness amongst a rising professional class, uninterested in the problems of poverty, no longer recognizing the working class let alone doing anything to help it. This time Trump has started taking over a Republican party that was working smoothly with Clintonian Democrats for a quarter century, managing to steer its supporters toward a path not questioning the hollowness of multiculturalism but heading them off in a parallel universe of Christian righteousness.

All that is over now. Electoral firewalls seem like firewalls only until their last manifestation, and in retrospect seem like flammable tinder; had Trump been allowed to talk about the issues, and nothing but, even if in his authoritarian way, and had he had the discipline to pivot quickly to his message despite being baited, the Democratic midwestern firewall, for example, might have easily crumbled. In any event, Trumpism is here to stay; what will the neoliberal elites do next?

Why Did Donald Trump Win?

There have always been two narratives about this election. One predicted what actually happened in the end, while the other missed the boat completely.

Narrative 1. Bernie Sanders represents the unachievable in American politics. Hillary Clinton is the candidate of experience and realism. Donald Trump is a temporary phenomenon, feeding on passions and resentments, not meant to last the duration. Trump's supporters are more economically privileged than Clinton and Sanders voters, and are motivated by pure racism and misogyny. The election is about the cultural values of tolerance, openness, and identity, therefore we must support Hillary. Anyone who doesn't support Hillary must be suspect of harboring racist and misogynist feelings themselves.

Narrative 2. Bernie Sanders is offering necessary correctives, at the most minimal level, to the excesses of the neoliberal economy of the past forty years. Hillary Clinton represents the essence of said neoliberalism, embodying its worst practices, from trade to immigration. Donald Trump has tapped into real economic anxiety amongst those—half of the country at least—who have lost under neoliberal globalization. This election is about returning equal economic rights to all citizens. Only Bernie Sanders has the winning message for this explosive situation.

Everyone who propagated Narrative 1—which is nearly 100% of the liberal media, the intellectual community as a whole, and elite professionals—got it wrong every step of the way. The utter failure of predictive power means that the model was flawed.

Those who believed in Narrative 2—which included a vanishingly small proportion of intellectuals—got it right at every turn. Trump won, Hillary lost, and we are in for a very bad time, just as our model predicted. Slavoj Žižek had it right, Michael Moore had it right, and I had been saying all along that this outcome was inevitable. I wrote back in May that Trump would win by pinning neoliberal failures squarely on Hillary's shoulders.

Essentially, those who chose Hillary over Bernie during the primaries, when we had a clear choice, voted for Trump, since Bernie was always the stronger candidate against Trump or any Republican general election candidate. The polls consistently proved it.

The liberal elite, all during this campaign, showed its intolerant colors, mocking anyone who raised questions about Hillary's background and competence as inherently misogynist, sidelining questions of political economy in favor of preferred identity politics tropes, banning dissenters and skeptics of Narrative 1 from their websites and forums, questioning their very humanity. Even now—in the wake of the Trump win—they are refusing to accept their culpability in making the wrong choice by throwing up their hands and exclaiming: "I can't understand how this could have happened!"

On a Pacifica radio show on October 27,[1] where I discussed the reasons why Trumpism had come into being and why I expected it to last well beyond the election regardless of the outcome, half the callers repeated the neoliberal Narrative 1, saying, in essence, that Trump supporters were facing undesirable economic fates because of their own lack of responsibility toward their personal lives. Why don't they get educated, why don't they get jobs, why don't they move to where the jobs are? And why wasn't I talking about the *Access Hollywood* tape—apparently the paramount issue in this campaign? Why didn't I talk about Trump's misogyny, which was instantly disqualifying and branded his supporters too as falling in the same vein? This was from Pacifica listeners, presumably the most liberal audience in America!

But there was also the other half, believers of Narrative 2, who thought that the Democratic party had been suicidal by not choosing Bernie, and who understood the economic grievances of the "leftovers" who supported Trump on the Republican side and Bernie on the Democratic side. They were not falling for the moral righteousness of the liberal media.

What can we say now about the fate of the entities involved in this crash of an election, when the contradictions have so manifestly come to the fore?

---

[1] The Living Art show of October 27, 2016, archived at http://kpft.org/archive/.

1. Is Neoliberalism Dead? Hardly. This is the ideology that survived 9/11, the presidency of George Bush Jr., and the Great Recession, with barely a scratch. But it has received its most serious blow yet (the first, less severe one, was Brexit), as its entire range of practices, from neoliberal trade benefiting large corporations to a kind of exploitative identity politics that favors internalization of neoliberal psychology, has come under attack from Trumpism. We shall see how neoliberalism responds and regroups, how it works through the Democratic party to find a different channel of expression than the Clintonian one.

2. Is the Democratic Party Dead? Given a clear progressive choice in the primaries, the Democratic party establishment went for the failed neoliberal candidate of war, inequality, and injustice. At the moment, the entire party stands discredited. It is not easy to write off a behemoth as powerful as this, but it is more vulnerable than it has been since the 1960s. The philosophy of catering to upwardly mobile professionals, exploiting immigrants in the neoliberal setup while simultaneously expounding their virtues, and constructing a façade of moral righteousness while ignoring the existence of poor people of any color, stands discredited. After their catastrophic loss in 2008, the Republicans went through one more cycle of doubling down, with Mitt Romney in 2012, before a populist revolution swept the establishment away. How long will it take the Democratic party as we knew it to end?

3. Is the Republican Party Dead? Clearly, it is not what it was before Trumpism, it is no longer the party of Reagan and other supply-siders. On paper at least Trumpism is virulently opposed to the principles of neoliberalism, around which Republicans, with minor differences on taxation and welfare and other policies, cohere with Democrats as a governing philosophy. To what extent will Trump put his anti-trade, anti-immigration, and anti-interventionist policies into practice? Even if he draws back on his stated goals, the genie is out of the bottle. The Republican party, exploiting cultural fears (exactly as the Democrats have done on the other side) while executing economic policies that benefit the rich, can no longer exist in its old form.

4. Is the Liberal Media Dead? One of the positives of this campaign is that despite relentless 24/7 propaganda about Trump, exaggerating his personal foibles while painting anyone not supportive of Hillary as a closet misogynist, racist, or even sexual predator, the message failed to get through. In the end, no one paid any attention. Those inside the elite bubble were persuaded that they were headed for victory, hearing nothing contrary in their own ecosphere, when they were in fact doomed. The people have shown that they can tune out this noise. The media has fragmented so much that only those who are already persuaded come within the ambit of any new message, so in essence they have pounded their way into their own irrelevance.

Enough deaths, I guess. I want to say that this feels eerily, and gloomily, like the outcome of election 2000, when every idealistic hope that young people had constructed, in the wake of the Bill Bradley and Ralph Nader campaigns, vanished into thin air, never to be seen again.
We regressed massively at that time, all talk of privacy and individualism, community and preventive health care, reparations and debt forgiveness, and international justice adjudication, disappearing forever. In 2008, Obama, with control of both houses of Congress, could have immediately resolved the immigration issue once and for all, or alleviated the misery of those burdened by housing and student debt, but he followed a strictly neoliberal governing philosophy, catering only to the banks and big corporations. (In a way, election 2016 is payback from the white working-class for everything Obama failed to pursue as a possibility in his two terms.)
Now, in 2016, at a minimum, following the Sanders revolt, we should have been talking in the context of the next administration about a $20 minimum wage, free college, Medicare for all, and a liberal, humane, twenty-first century immigration policy to live up to our ideals. Instead, we are going to regress almost a century in our attitudes to corporations, migrants, working conditions, taxation, welfare, the environment, and healthcare. We should be talking at this point, a decade after the financial collapse, about a transcendent alternative to failed capitalist practices which are not in tune with current levels of science and technology, but instead we are backsliding at an apocalyptic pace toward primitive levels of discourse.
At each stage of crisis, neoliberalism has gifted us with a serious regression to the past. Now we face the most serious regression of all.
In the 1930s, facing another economic crisis, America—unlike Europe—chose the path of liberal universalism, a preliminary welfare

state that admitted the existence of poverty and misery. This time, following Europe, we have chosen a proto-fascist, or at least extreme right-wing authoritarian, path. We can trace this deadly outcome directly to the inability of the governing elites to steadily refuse to do anything about extreme inequality; Clinton, during the primaries, mocked free college and single-payer healthcare, saying it would never happen. Even a rhetorical concession to a $15 minimum wage by the candidate of the elites was too much.

The people who will suffer dramatically in the coming days are immigrants in general, and Muslims in particular, since they are the most defenseless of all the targeted constituencies. Everyone else has their defenders in the establishment, but not this group of people. To all those who made the cynical choice of supporting Hillary Clinton, when the evidence was clear that she would perform much worse than Bernie Sanders against Trump or any other Republican, thank you for causing this catastrophe. You are directly responsible for the desperate fate of millions of people about to undergo unimaginable hardship, while you talk cavalierly of moving to Canada or Europe. Keep talking, in your bubble.

Forty Short Post-Election Theses:
Where Do We Stand Now and Where Do We Go from Here?

1. Do not underestimate Trump's executive ability. He ran at least five different campaigns during this one cycle, showing himself swift-footed and quickly able to change staff and ideas depending on the needs of the moment. He will move blindingly fast to enact his repressive agenda, every word of which he meant seriously.

2. Trump's marketing strategy was to formulate a message based on anxieties that already existed, instead of shoving a preexisting ideology down people's throats. As important as the economic anxiety was the populace's resistance to liberal political correctness.

3. The monopoly of political correctness over the media and the intellectual apparatus has had dire results, it has reached its end point in the fascistic reaction. Political correctness diverts attention from the kinds of material issues that propel this kind of election result. How can this monopoly by broken?

4. When democracy on the left is suppressed—i.e., someone like Bernie Sanders is cheated out of the nomination that should have been his—the result is an extreme reaction from the right, and the victory of the opposite of the suppressed message. This has been true for nearly forty years of neoliberalism.

5. Fascism arises only when liberalism fails. How has liberalism failed us? The cultural liberalism of the elites doesn't allow room for economic liberalism, which has been sidelined during the course of the neoliberal ascendancy.

6. Trump has rewritten all the rules of politics. Those in the elite bubble, both Republicans and Democrats, have been made to look like fools. Trump made a direct appeal to the people, converting American politics into a reality show. Politics is reality TV now, and will remain so. How does a rational message of economic redistribution and justice get through this screen?

7. The Democratic party insisted on nominating a scandalous candidate not because they are stupid but because they wanted to preserve neoliberalism at all costs. This is why the entire party establishment fell in line, it was more important to protect neoliberalism than stop fascism. They deliberately gambled with the future of the country and lost.

8. The demographic wall has been shattered. Trump's only chance of success was to break through in the Rust Belt, as the Democrats' weakest point of exposure. Ted Cruz or any conventional Republican would not have won, the demographic wall would have stood. The only way was to scramble the map. Has the Rust Belt been breached for good? Yes, if fortune favors Trump and he can deliver even a small amount of what he promised.

9. Just as the neoliberal elites were gambling, the electorate took a massive gamble too, they chose to end unbearable stagnation under neoliberalism, even at the risk of bringing on something apocalyptic. They knew the risks, but they could not bear neoliberal precariousness anymore.

10. The elites had a chance to figure out an amiable solution to inequality, to share the fruits of the biggest economy in the world. They didn't, and now it's de facto civil war. Things cannot go back to the status quo ante, the elite consensus has collapsed for good.

11. The Democratic party has been completely hollowed out at every level after a quarter-century of Clinton/Obama neoliberalism. The house, senate, governorships, and state legislatures are all gone. The presidential firewall at last collapsed, because in the end you cannot lose offices at every other level yet keep just the presidency.

12. Why didn't Hillary select Bernie for vice president? This would have guaranteed a win. Even choosing Elizabeth Warren would have ensured support from economic liberals. Sticking to neoliberalism down to the last point of contention was more important than securing a win. Was she planning to keep her word on anything she promised Bernie on policy? Why would millennials believe her or anyone in the corporate wing of the party in the future?

13. The millennials are up for grabs. The discredited Democrats don't have them. African Americans, Hispanics, and Asians are also up for grabs, if Trump does something magnanimous in their interest, which is highly unlikely—but potentially the Democrats can lose them in a new realignment.

14. The liberals' only strategy was to attack Trump personally, which failed. People are not that gullible, which is to their credit.

15. This election result goes back to 9/11 and the consequent American violence against innocent Middle Eastern people. This is the boomerang effect. When you start imperialist wars, and violate the norms of humanity, in the end it comes back to haunt you. The explosive situation created outside is replicated at home. We never resolved the war crimes of the Bush administration, that was an absolute no-go area for Obama. We kept playing with fire, with perpetual war abroad and terrorist fears constantly inflamed even eight years after Bush. This never-ending global chess game, killing people at will when our fancy strikes, is integrally connected with the Trump win.

16. Note the terrorist events that occurred around the world like a metronomic beat all throughout the election campaign, propping up Trump's law and order message at moments of key vulnerability, and which have now ceased all of a sudden as Trump regroups.

17. This is the perfect bookend to election 2000, when the media was in the tank for Bush II, desperately wanting him to be president. They are reaping the results of what they sowed then: the illiteracy, dumbness, irrationality, and catering to the basest fears and instincts. Given who they are, they will draw all the wrong "lessons" from this debacle, and try to perpetuate their ignorance.

18. By not taking the slightest steps to address economic inequality, neoliberals have plunged us into the abyss. Whenever we want even the slightest concessions, as in 2000, the system gives us something ten times more repressive to set us back. It is a system-wide failure, it is not just a failure of either political party. Trump is who we are, it is where we are, it is who we want to be, just as Bush was all those things to at least half the population.

19. Trump, masterful strategist that he is, saw two bankrupt political parties, and seized control of one, as in his real estate dealings. Who will seize control of the bankrupt Democratic party now?

20. A new political consensus will emerge eventually, though it may take a while. Both parties are dead, the neoliberal consensus is over. This is the first stage of either an authoritarian/inegalitarian political economy or a participatory/egalitarian one. The false center is gone.

21. The neoliberal wing of the party had no intention of presenting any policy agenda, they were only prompted to concede a few things because of the pressure put by the Sanders wing. They have lost all credibility and should never be heard from again.

22. Only Bernie Sanders has the moral authority to lead the Democratic party. Already he is insisting on fighting Trump tooth and nail, while Clinton is nowhere to be seen.

23. Anyone who supports what the Clintons represent beyond this point doesn't deserve to be called a liberal.

24. Clinton offered efficient managerial stewardship of the assets of the propertied class, including young professionals, which includes wise stewardship of the empire. That was the sum total of her philosophy, and Obama's too. This turned out to be extremely divisive, because the nation is more than that. Others have different priorities than neoliberal economic success.

25. Writers, intellectuals, academics, and artists in the public eye are nearly 100% with "the Dems." When I was in college it was ridiculous to

be for the Dems. We were socialists, Marxists, radicals, anarchists, greens, freethinkers, rebels, secularists, hardcore feminists, utopians. What the hell happened to all of that? Young people should get away from the Dems, and build a green/socialist/egalitarian alternative, not just at the political party level but as a living reality, a transcendent goal of existence. Trump has done us a favor by blowing up the corporate Dems, they were never going to change on their own.

26. This should be the end of the intensely anti-intellectual "liberal" websites and blogs, right? We know who they are, shoveling pure snark at anyone the least bit skeptical of the party line, designed to flatter the hip and cool young professionals with politically correct propaganda and little understanding of the reality of working people. Young people should educate themselves about the history of political economy, stop wasting time with this diversionary new media.

27. Can we ever imagine Clinton or anyone from that side of the Democratic party touring Appalachia? The inner cities? Wherever the poor live? Not as a political stunt but with any degree of sincerity toward fellow citizens?

28. Hillary tried to make the last two months of the election, along with her supporters in the liberal media, a referendum on rape culture! That's just not where the country was for this election. Bernie would have never brought up this stuff, it would have been a pure contest of economic ideas, his sane proposals to reform trade and taxation and immigration, versus Trump's lunatic ones.

29. The only person on the planet Trump could have beaten was Hillary. The Democrats insisted on picking that one person.

30. Obama didn't even nominate a liberal justice the left could get excited about, he chose a bland corporate nobody supported in the past by Republicans, and now they want us to cry over impending supreme court losses! Before he announced the nomination, the Republicans had already declared opposition for the rest of his term, so he knew it would be a live issue until the end, possibly one that could have swung the election. Yet he chose not to exploit it.

31. The electorate wisely rejected 44 years of a Bush or a Clinton at or near the top, which it would have been by 2024.

32. We also come full circle in confronting the total decimation of the Democratic party in congress and at the state level under Clinton and Obama. The Democrats had a lock on the House since the New Deal, which they lost permanently in 1994, making any legislative advance impossible. This was a direct result of the Clinton neoliberal cave-in, it's what happens when you end opposition and turn your own party into a replica of the other side. Essentially, we've had one-party rule since the end of the Cold War. And this has created the philosophical vacuum Trump has stepped into.

33. In his first television appearance since the election, Bernie Sanders showed tremendous statesmanship,[1] by repeatedly telling Wolf Blitzer that we would not tolerate assaults on Muslims and immigrants. Any political leader who does not adopt the same level of opposition at this moment of reckoning is irrelevant to the future.

34. The entire Democratic party leadership should resign in shame. How does Howard Dean have the nerve to want to run for DNC chair after having opposed Sanders and having thrown in his lot with the Clinton machine for more than a decade? Sanders has the moral authority to have his choice, Keith Ellison, go forward. A new leadership and new philosophy of resistance needs to mobilize before Trump's inauguration, and before his anticipated dire first actions, particularly against immigrants. Can the party move that fast?

35. The ongoing street protests are exactly what's needed. They are the only thing that could stall Trump's intent toward immigrants and Muslims. Who will take up their cause? That's your future leadership right there.

36. Trump is coming after undocumented immigrants and Muslims in a big way. Mobilize *now*, be ready to fight. Every liberal institution rolled over in the first two years after 9/11, as registration of Muslims, illegal incarceration, mass deportations, and torture and rendition became the

---

[1] https://www.youtube.com/watch?v=olILIkiIrM0.

new order. Nothing happened in those first years as a token of liberal resistance. We will soon find out if this has changed.

37. Why didn't Tim Kaine debate Mike Pence on his radical policies? What if Trump's policies had been fully exposed instead of going after him as a sexual predator? Everything he plans to do in his first days was already out in public, why was this not the main focus? Kaine, another neoliberal Clinton acolyte, a former DNC chair during yet another decline, should be nowhere near the leadership.

38. Here come Fareed Zakaria and Jill Abramson and all the rest of the liberal prognosticators, blaming themselves for their failure to understand the agony of people in the rural areas. They are sorry they didn't go to the South. The South? They're right under your nose, in the urban areas, do you need to travel thousands of miles to find poor people?

39. Blaming poor white people for taking advantage of white privilege is another part of runaway political correctness. The poor white person is as subject to police and surveillance authority, as subject to arbitrary employer exploitation, as the poor person of any color. Can that meme end now?

40. A forceful seizure of the Democratic party is necessary, and at the moment only Bernie has the moral authority to do it. In the longer term, there must be electoral reform, campaign finance reform, space for third parties and viewpoints beyond the two centrist parties. But in the short-term, Bernie is the youngest seventy-five-year-old in the land, so take it away!

The Coming Immigration Crisis:
The First and Last Battle of the Trump Administration

It begins already, the struggle for the soul of the Democratic party.

It's hard to believe that the entire leadership of the party, which led to this electoral debacle, hasn't already resigned in shame. Why is Donna Brazile still there? Why are any of the people who shoved Clinton down our throats and showed themselves masters of ineptness at every turn of the game? In a responsible parliamentary system, they would be gone already, never to be heard from again. In our system, they are always planning their umpteenth comeback.

Bernie Sanders has endorsed progressive Minnesota congressman Keith Ellison as DNC chair. Only Sanders has come out of this election with his moral authority intact and even enhanced; everyone else is ruined. Howard Dean, much as I liked him in 2004, is not the right choice, because he went after Sanders and threw in his lot with the Clintonites as early as a decade ago.

This, the first post-Clinton struggle, will decide it right there. I hate to start with a discussion about the Democratic party leadership, because over two generations the party has been completely hollowed out as a vehicle for corporate interests; but those who are progressives, and there are a few left, ought to assert themselves vigorously in the tremendous vacuum that has suddenly emerged and prevent the rise of the Clintonites from the ashes.

The street protests that have been going on all over the country are the way to go, they are infinitely more important than anything that will happen in the halls of congress to set the trend. They are a roadblock—perhaps the most important one—to what is about to go down as soon as Trump takes over.

His very first executive actions will have to do with attacking vulnerable immigrants. When he suspends Obama's executive orders providing temporary relief and semi-legalization to the Dreamers, and when he instructs ICE to no longer abide by the policy of targeting criminal aliens for deportation and to go after everyone, even at the cost of breaking up long-established families, then many millions of people—the families and close friends of those directly affected—will be the first casualties of the Trump regime.

Sanders, in his first televised appearance after the election, and in appearances since then, has displayed tremendous statesmanship, the kind that I do not yet see from others in the Democratic party establishment. He has repeatedly mentioned Muslims and undocumented immigrants, and said that attacks on them will not be tolerated. Whoever shows this kind of leadership, within the party or outside, ought to emerge as the natural political leaders.

Could we ever expect Clinton to come out and say something so unequivocal in defending the human rights of those most vulnerable amongst us? Is she plotting her next machinations, even as her bloated staff comes up with excuse after excuse for the loss (blame FBI director Jim Comey, when you know that in every election momentum breaks in one direction or another in the last few days), so that the only real explanation, the ill-fit of their ideological message with the electorate's needs, is hidden and shoved under the rug.

Both the struggle for the leadership of the Democratic party and the protests on the streets are good signs of mobilization against Trump's imminent assault on civil liberties and human rights. Any moves on trade or foreign policy or taxation will take a bit longer to work their way through, but expect a complete repeal of the Obama legacy on immigration, half-hearted as it was, as soon as Trump takes power.

The time to mobilize and prepare is now, in these next two months. I hope the protests escalate and spread everywhere, and that a set of specific demands is made and endorsed by civil liberties organizations, to hold the next president accountable from the start.

Let us note that during the savagely repressive fascistic stage of the Bush administration, between September 2001 and March 2003, civil society was completely powerless and absent. Registration of specific groups of aliens, mass deportations, illegal incarceration, unlawful surveillance, and torture and rendition, all became instituted as permanent policies of the U.S. government, policies that have not been fully contested to this day. Educators, healthcare professionals, lawyers, everyone in the front lines who could have opposed such policies—such as the specific targeting of foreign students at American universities, or

Muslim visitors to the country—took a pass, and were not heard from until the Bush administration lost political legitimacy, years later.

If we have a repeat of this situation in the assault on immigrants that is about to take place next January, then all will be lost; it will be possible for Trump to carry out the rest of his agenda, from destroying healthcare rights to environmental equity, without pause. Immigration will be the first and last battle of the Trump administration, just as the passage of the Patriot Act, which took place with near complete complicity of all the Democrats in Congress, was the first and last battle of the Bush administration after 9/11.

As Nixon followed Johnson, and as Bush followed Clinton, expect the unimaginable worst from Trump, then multiply it a hundred times; that's what we're going to get, do not expect any moderation or civility when it comes to exposed groups of people. One possible strategy for Trump might be to enact something like the dreaded Sensenbrenner law (of 2005), making unpersons of all immigrants with unresolved status issues; simply state that anyone with outstanding issues who doesn't come forward by a certain date will be permanently barred from legalization, thereby dissolving millions of such persons with one stroke of the pen. A registration program forcing people to expose themselves would accomplish the same purpose.

The people Trump will bring on are so far on the fringes that Bush would never have considered them (just as Bush's people would have been radical lunatics for Nixon). Senator Jeff Sessions of Alabama, perhaps the most influential white supremacist in this country, has been nominated to take over the Department of Justice. Senator Sessions single-handedly blocked the Bush administration's generous immigration reform bills of 2006 and 2007. He's been licking his chops ever since to end immigration altogether, including birthright citizenship. Also influential in designing anti-immigrant policy will be Kansas Secretary of State Kris Kobach, who implemented a registry for Muslims during the Bush administration, and is one of the fiercest xenophobes in the country.

This is what we are facing. Most likely, it will not be established organizations like the ACLU which will make strong headway against an assault so radical, but spontaneous eruptions (like Occupy or BLM) that will pick up the baton; but we will see who retains credibility.

Let us remember that President Obama kept in place the entire illegal surveillance and repression apparatus instituted by the Bush administration. As each Democrat succeeds a repressive Republican, under the neoliberal regime we have experienced for the last forty-plus years, the previous administration's repressive apparatus is retained and legitimized, and keeps growing and growing.

The total lack of interest in holding anyone from the Bush administration accountable for crimes against humanity will end up being the most haunting legacy of the Obama era; he explicitly guaranteed, right from the start, that there would be no reconciliation and accountability, there would be no looking back at past crimes. Not only that, but Obama took some of the crudeness out of the illegalities, and turned them to more postmodern expression: the drone wars which he accelerated and established as a foundation of foreign policy, the targeted assassinations which are illegal by definition but happen now as preemptive "liberal" initiatives: war as media game, war as recessive and invisible, taken to a whole new level.

For nearly all of his first term Obama was in full-blown appeasement mode. He refused to advance any progressive goals while having control of both houses of Congress, and was obsessed with cutting a grand bargain on debt and putting social security on the chopping block. His first three years were an unprecedented era of deportations, succeeded by half-hearted measures providing semi-relief to selective groups of immigrants, rather than providing blanket protection, when Latino turnout was necessary to win the 2012 election. In any event, the whole Obama legacy, from executive orders on the environment to immigration protections, is about to be repealed.

While the Clinton machine made fun of Trump's business acumen, the evidence, to the contrary, is right before our eyes. One could write a book on Trump's brilliant executive decision-making during the course of his impossible win. He ran at least three different general election campaigns, quickly responding to changing circumstances, never hesitating to correct course and to bring on new sets of people and ideas. He launched his campaign years ago, identifying the unaddressed needs of the electorate and formulating his message according to existing market desires and then having the skills to get the product out despite "liberal" media resistance.

As far as immigration goes, he has converted a protofascist ideology, borrowed from European and older American precedents, into a nativist/populist movement that can quickly dissolve decades of failing identity politics clusters on the liberal side. In other words, he has all the executive skills necessary to alter the political balance for good. Unless, that is, civil society recognizes his skill and moves swiftly to exceed his capabilities by offering a full-throated defense of liberties.

We are facing an imminent crisis on immigration because Democrats chose to keep this issue alive—as a tool in the culture wars—rather than resolving it. Hillary Clinton was planning in 2008 to extend the Iraq and Afghanistan wars, perhaps start a new war with Iran, and privatize social security. In 2016, until pushed by the Sanders insurgency to make some rhetorical concessions, to which she had no allegiance, she was planning to run a campaign completely empty of ideas. The reason why the entire focus was on mocking Trump and his supporters as racist and misogynist was because neoliberalism could not have entered the arena of ideas under her reign. Both parties had planned for a prefabricated Jeb Bush-Hillary Clinton neoliberal contest, discussing the minutiae of "entitlement" reform or the degree to which tax concessions should help corporations, and ignore poor and vulnerable populations altogether.

The only thing that can counter Trump's executive ability to push through his regressive agenda on taxation, welfare, the environment, and above all immigration, likely to be his first line of battle, is a clear progressive vision that needs to be articulated now and hammered at consistently from this point on.

What we do know is that political correctness has failed as rhetoric and as strategy, and will not help the cause of immigrants. Political correctness is not the way to defend immigrant rights or the rights of any other targeted population during the coming assault.

Note that during the height of the Bush administration assault on immigrants, minorities, and gays, politically correct rhetoric was likewise at its peak, not least from administration officials. Identity politics says, Defend me because I am different than you, protect my rights because they come from a special place, leave me alone because in the end I am incomprehensible to you as the other. Whereas a defense of rights based on universalism, something that suffered a precipitous decline during the Clinton/Obama era of the last quarter-century, rests on tolerance not as a special privilege granted to one discrete entity after another but as the foundation of society, something that stems not from the separateness of each group in the cultural sphere but the similarity of everyone in the legal realm.

I would argue that liberal tolerance rests on an understanding of class, whereas political correctness, i.e., contemporary multiculturalism, is founded on ending class rhetoric. Human rights flow from recognition of class, not its avoidance. Political correctness—which manifested in the latter stages of the campaign in the form of depicting Trump's supporters as would-be sexual predators and upholders of white privilege—is divisive, and does not engender support for minority rights under a rubric that can cut across lines of color and origin.

Half the country, that which voted for Trump, is inflamed by the strategy of political correctness to defend minority rights. They are bothered by the insane degree to which speech codes make a fetish of particular identity groups, but whose proponents are revealed as hypocritical in their simultaneous mockery of the baseline offset, the despised other, i.e., the supposed inheritors of white privilege, against whom each identity group asserts difference and moral superiority.

We ought to listen to this part of the country as we set about defending immigrant and minority rights, because despite all the fears about Trump representing an ascendancy of xenophobia, let it be noted that three quarters of voters in exit polls this election favored a path to citizenship for undocumented immigrants; the country overwhelmingly, still, rejects deportation. That generosity does not come from identity politics. It comes from forgotten liberal principles, shared values of economic justice, that need to be recovered—and soon.

Quit America!
The Case for Moral Disengagement from American Politics

"There are a lot of killers. What, you think our country's so innocent?" — Donald J. Trump, Feb. 6, 2017

There continues to be a gross underestimation, even amongst politically aware liberals, of what we are really up against, and how to counter it. Increasingly, our fellow citizens are resorting to the concepts of fascism to describe the current situation, but this is not necessarily followed by any cogent reflection on what the political subject under fascism needs to do. Ordinary liberal prescriptions have no chance of success under a regime that has moved into an overt fascist mode; moreover, the unacknowledged continuities from the recent neoliberal past, which led to the fascist overture in the first place, mar any consistency of thought amongst intellectuals, activists, and ordinary citizens.

The time has come to explore modes of existence that only make sense under a fascist regime, or rather, they are the only modes that make sense under fascist conditions. Above all, the question of moral disengagement from any existing political practice must be taken seriously, and this includes so-called "resistance." Are there things that pass under the activist rubric today that are actually strengthening rather than weakening fascism? If that is the case, then those activities must undergo severe scrutiny, because it may well be that what seems like activism is actually passivism, and vice versa.

I started writing about a "soft" American totalitarianism for the first time in 1998, in the wake of the Monica Lewinsky scandal. American civic institutions seemed to me to have stopped functioning for the first time in 1994, after the Gingrich takeover, which made me take a step back, only to reemerge, awakened, when the Lewinsky scandal happened. I was not interested in the content of the scandal, which was a mere pretext to engineer reaction in a form we had never seen before without the instrument of twenty-four-hour cable news, but the way in which perceptions were being manipulated seemed to me to be mortally dangerous for democracy.

After 9/11, I resorted to the vocabulary of fascism for that whole decade, often comparing and contrasting Bush's early years to the Hitlerian model, since this was what I knew best then. However, once I started studying Italian fascism seriously about seven years ago, it has seemed to me that the original Mussolinian model is more apt, because of some important missing elements in the way fascism has been developing in this country. During the 2016 election campaign, I identified points of similarity between Trump and Mussolini, and considered whether he was better seen as a fascist or a populist authoritarian. Clearly, in the time since he took over he has entered an overtly fascist stage, with elements of both Mussolini and Hitler in play.

But I think that instead of these admittedly helpful historical comparisons it might be more clarifying now to conceptualize a new form of fascism: the third important variant, if you will, following the original Mussolini model and the later Hitlerian model, which was a development of and departure from the original in many respects.

Italy was a weak state, certainly militarily so, and had been undergoing serious strife between labor and capital in the years immediately preceding Mussolini's takeover; when Mussolini asserted Italy's grievances against the so-called "plutocratic powers" (above all Great Britain and France), he was arguing from a position of weakness. Germany was a much stronger state, obviously, in the military, economic, and cultural sense, but Hitler's aim was also to become the world's greatest power, even if starting from a position much stronger than Italy's. America, when it started going down the fascist route (I would say coinciding with the termination of the cold war), was already the world's undisputed dominant power, arguably stronger than the Roman and British empires ever were at their peak. Starting with the Bush II regime, and now accelerated manifold in the Trump regime, American fascism has been pleading irresolvable grievances (against internal and external abusers) from a position of unparalleled strength! That is a remarkable deviance from past fascist models, and it changes everything.

Furthermore, I would argue that everything Trump has done so far or plans to do fits perfectly well within the neoliberal model, whether it's massive tax cuts for corporations, cutting back social security, Medicare, and essential social services, privatizing healthcare, converting infrastructure building to an essentially privatized domain, and certainly repressing immigrants by driving them underground or expelling them. All of it is a continuation, if an acceleration, of neoliberal practices familiar from more than thirty-five years of governance. The only thing that stands out so far is pulling out from the Trans-Pacific Partnership (TPP), and making noises about renegotiating NAFTA, but the latter hasn't happened yet and is not likely to in any substantial way, and the former was in deep trouble anyway, a hodgepodge of conflicting corporate monopolies amongst the negotiating countries that didn't seem to be going anywhere even before Trump withdrew. I suspect that on trade the classic neoliberal position will soon assert itself, and it may be worth taking a pass on trade for a while, from the neoliberal point of view, as long as other elements of the agenda get a radical boost.

So I would argue that if we're seeing fascism, it is a peculiar form of fascism indeed, because it looks like one hundred percent neoliberalism from where I am. Nonetheless, it is fascism of a kind, it is neoliberalism's fascist mode. Modern capitalism has a tendency to keep falling into the fascist style from time to time, and this became inevitable for us once the Soviet Union fell and there was no ideological check on American capitalism. The equations became imbalanced, there was excessive power which had nowhere to flow, and it was destined to go this way and it has.

What is truly unfortunate is that globalization's reform elements—I mean international action on human rights issues such as the environment, agricultural equity, urban poverty, medical care, the price of drugs, indebtedness and servitude, and war crimes—were all on the agenda in the late 1990s, but the onset of overt fascism in America made the entire world, particularly Europe, put these global civilizational issues on the back-burner. Europe was trending strongly toward global cosmopolitanism, which might have ended up being a transitionary stage toward worldwide democratic socialism, but America, in resurrecting an imaginary global Islamic enemy for the past twenty years (recall that the first Osama bin Laden video surfaced in 1998, and that Clinton's launch of missiles against this protagonist's alleged strongholds in Afghanistan and Sudan also occurred in the year of Lewinsky), has probably irrevocably damaged the global cosmopolitan agenda.

Citizenship, throughout the 1990s, after the Soviet Union ended as a theoretical pole, was being reconceptualized as transnational, contingent, and fluid, a right not tied to nationalism, which was a radical change that had been awaited by the world's enlightened thinkers for more than two hundred years. It was the ultimate promise of liberalism being slowly fulfilled, but sadly, because of the rise of American fascism, it was not to be. That dream is all but dead now. Europe, taking its cues from America, has vastly retreated on immigrant rights, refugee and asylum claims, and human rights administration even within the European Union.

The question for those currently mounting a resistance, aside from its inherent limitations (even Gandhi with his "successful" salt march of 1930 and other civil disobedience actions didn't see much significant results, it took the collapse of the British empire after World War II for India to finally gain independence), is what it is that American liberal activists are trying to get back *to*.

First, the Republican party, under Ronald Reagan, became the prime transmitter of neoliberalism. Then, once Clinton transformed the Democratic party, both parties became equal bearers of neoliberal ideology. So what is the aspiration to return to? The Democratic party under Obama? It was an ideal carrier of neoliberalism, in every area of governance one can think of. No doubt Trump wants to exert existing immigration powers to a genocidal level, and he will, but the powers were granted to him under the neoliberal administrations of Clinton and Obama, and fortified by additional powers sought by Bush II.

Clinton's 1996 anti-immigrant legislation was arguably the most draconian American immigration law ever passed (for example, in retroactively punishing legal residents for minor crimes, henceforth called "aggravated felonies," providing the authority to expel immigrants who had lived here for decades, and enshrining the loathsome concept of expedited removals, meaning deportation without judicial hearings), and likewise Obama continued the "enforcement"-first policy, for example by deputizing state and local authorities to act as immigration police. Everything Trump wants to do to embark on his ethnic cleansing campaign has been gifted to him by neoliberal presidents of either party.

And aside from the repression of immigrants, who have been living under a reign of terror since 1996, what else do we want to go back to? The fascist Trumpian reaction occurred only because neoliberalism set up a situation of economic inequality that was completely unsustainable. When less than ten people own more wealth than half the world's population, that is not a situation that can lead to any good outcome; it simply cannot be perpetuated beyond a certain point, as we are seeing in the collapse of American democracy today.

The petty bourgeois liberals who so eagerly supported Hillary Clinton, and were so adamant against Bernie Sanders's meager demands on behalf of aspirational millennials for a modicum of democratic socialist reforms, will be relieved to know that Tom Perez, Barack Obama's labor secretary and Hillary Clinton's potential vice-presidential nominee, an exemplary neoliberal, has managed to defeat Sanders's choice, Keith Ellison, a true progressive who would have started setting the Democratic party on a different path. We are talking about a democratic revolution as the price worthy of participating in American social and political life at this dangerous juncture, and we can't even get the Democratic party chairman who is the choice of the candidate who would have soundly defeated Trump!

Fascism always comes about because of the failures of liberalism. Sometimes these failures are exaggerated, as was true before the Mussolini ascendancy, but in the American case all the data says that for the health and well-being of the people, neoliberalism over the last thirty-five years has been a colossal failure. Thus the polity, at least since the 1990s, has been wishing death upon itself, as evidenced in the most successful Hollywood productions and other creations of popular culture. Had Hillary Clinton not announced her candidacy, there would have been no Bernie Sanders, and certainly no candidate Trump; but this is not to blame Hillary, she is merely representative of where the Democratic party, that is to say the liberal establishment, is: when they had the chance during the primaries, the entire party establishment supported Hillary over Bernie. Though they may be suppressing their true leanings for the moment, under the onslaught of a storm that promises to take down every American's security, property, and investments, one senses the Hillary supporters ready to take the fight to the Sanders camp, as soon as the opportunity presents itself again.

The Democratic party today is a fairly accurate reflection of where the country's liberal institutions, from broadcasting and arts and media organizations, to the sensibility in the academy and government at all levels, pretty much rests: focusing on an exaggerated concept of personal responsibility, which is at the least neoliberal and at its worst fascistic. The publishing industry, my own personal bailiwick, operates entirely within the neoliberal paradigm, as I know from twenty years of experience; the well-known American publishing houses are simply extensions of the same thinking that infects CNN or any media organization, a mindset that can neither name the ideology it perpetuates (neoliberalism), nor mount any democratic resistance against it.

To agree with my case for moral disengagement, you would have to be persuaded that each effort of engagement, from activism to voting to articulation of demands of any sort, makes the situation worse rather than better. If participation leaves things unchanged, then it may not be enough of a case for disengagement; if participation, including voting, makes things better, then no doubt my case is invalidated.

My argument has to do not with the scope of what needs to happen—just think of the intolerable situation with regard to totalitarian-style gerrymandering, the influence of the billionaire class on campaigns, or the rabid exclusion of third parties, all of which guarantee neoliberal hegemony—but the logic of American fascism: to resist it, in any form whatsoever, only makes it stronger.

When there was a tiny bit of protest, in the form of the Naderite antiglobalization campaign in 1999-2000, we got George W. Bush; after eight intolerable years of Obama's neoliberalism, which worsened inequality on a frightening scale, the only thing the Sanderite protest got us was Trump. Essentially, neoliberalism is saying, be quiet and accept things as they are, or we will give you something much, much worse. And that's where we are today, once again, as some of us, shell-shocked already, look back with nostalgia to the years of Obama, Clinton, and even Bush II.

Fascist formalities have become instrumentalized, under neoliberal hegemony, as the means to suppress demands for equality. Fascism's forms are ever-present, deriving strength from collective belief in American ideals, occurring again and again, and with stronger and stronger force, incarnated at will.

For things to get better, there would have to be nothing less than a democratic revolution, because the situation before, as I explained, was only slow death, a silent strangling that would have continued under a Hillary Clinton presidency: the same terrorist oppression of immigrants, the same radical exclusion of poor, uneducated people of any color from the "meritocracy," all of it couched in the respectable language of neoliberal personal responsibility, unlike Trump's crude expostulation of the same basic ideology in overt fascist terminology. The Democratic party would have to cease to exist as the ideal neoliberal vehicle for the resistance to be said to have worked; is that even possible to conceive? Other than Sanders, I do not know of any member of congress who is not beholden to neoliberalism in its essence. There would have to be room for true democratic expression, including for democratic socialism, whether under third parties or a rejuvenated progressive wing of the Democratic party.

All of this is so far from the realm of possibility, under normal modes of activism, that the imagination comes up short. On the contrary, the typical forms of resistance, accepting the neoliberal order as given, only worsen the undemocratic nature of our polity. After eight years of activism and resistance under Obama, what have we accomplished? At the state and local levels, more overtly fascist politicians are in control in almost unprecedented numbers, recalling earlier segregationist eras. Human rights, particularly immigrant rights, are more compromised by far than they were at the beginning of the Obama administration. The same goes for any measure of democracy or equality.

Civil resistance, in order for it to work, must escalate gradually; marches and protests are fine, but this is pretty much the level where the liberal activists seem comfortable. Will there be escalating general strikes? The strike announced for February 17 encountered immediate resistance from those amongst the petty bourgeoisie; they are said to be fighting a new Hitler, but they cannot imagine taking a day off from work, which would interfere with their routine "obligations"; weekend protests with friends are fine. In order for civil resistance to work, people have to put their bodies on the line, have to court mass arrests, have to gum up the works and grind down the machinery of fascist oppression to a halt. We are simply not up for the challenge, despite what some naïve citizens still think of as the main weapon on our side: the internet. If we are up against a true Hitler, who has the National Guard at his beck and call and who has already signed executive orders to implement mass deportations by decree, then the internet is of little help; it makes us feel better to vent, but that is about it.

Of course, I could be wrong about all this, and it could be that resistance leads Trump to have second thoughts, makes civil servants across the government push back vigorously against fascism, and revives both the Democratic and Republican parties to go back to their respective liberal and conservative roots rather than the two-headed neoliberal monster they've become. We could have a mass movement of compassion toward immigrants, Muslims, and poor and unhealthy people in this country. The media could become a repository of diverse opinion. We could see mass support for disengagement from our wars in the

Middle East and retreat from our worldwide assault on human rights. Of course, all of that could happen, in which case, go ahead, participate, engage, remain hopeful that we can go back to the thing that we've lost, or make it even better, and I will accept that I'm wrong.

But I know that there is nothing to hope for from our entire (neoliberal) intellectual establishment; how can there be a chance for resistance to work in that situation? They, the country's thinkers, especially those who consider themselves progressive, are the conveyors of the virus that has led to fascism. We are not yet ready to give up empire (we call it our "world standing"), and therefore the fascism that goes with it; we just want a nice human face on it, an Obama or a reformed Hillary Clinton.

Why do I think that resistance makes fascism worse? Because it creates the illusion, for a while (as under the Obama administration), that things are getting better, but they only get worse. Resistance legitimizes, and fascism, especially, thrives on it. The two missing elements in the Bushian version of fascism were the lack of a charismatic leader and the potential of a fascist militia, the first of which has at last come true and the second of which now seems a real possibility. I would say that it's because America is fascist but also the world's strongest power, and administratively already possesses total capacity to destroy any entity, internally and externally, the way it wants to, that resistance only strengthens the fascist regime because it gives it something to fight against. Fascism needs an enemy to build itself against, but what if the enemy were to retreat and disappear? What would it fight against?

Again, what is there to go back to, if in fact the aim of the resistance is to recapture what we have lost? The liberal intelligentsia, for fifteen years, has been convulsed with identity politics; in these early days of the renewed anti-Muslim and anti-Latino genocide we're witnessing, what has saved, to the extent that anything has, immigrant lives? The judiciary, going back to constitutional principles, which has nothing to do with identity politics.

We are possibly witnessing the implosion of American capitalism (i.e., neoliberalism) and hopefully the empire as well, while liberals, those who are protesting today, did not protest the mass incarceration and forceful expulsion of individuals who had been in this country for decades, did not protest the drone wars and illegal killings and fomenting of civil wars and mass displacement under our auspices ever since 9/11. The Obama presidency is destined to go down in history as a footnote; we are simply picking up fascist steam now from where we left off in 2003, before the Iraq War started going awry. The world war that began on 9/11 has resumed, we never left it in the intervening years, because we never sought accountability.

It is all too easy, as many liberals are doing today, to experience nostalgia for Bush the younger, but every fascistic impulse Trump is expressing today was fully manifest in the early Bush II years; that was the truly horrifying era that we, as a nation, never really wanted to account for and reconcile, when we embarked on illegal surveillance, torture, and detention. There is not an external enemy to fight, the enemy is all the liberal institutions (which in a perverse way Trump is saying too), the enemy is all of us who have implicitly supported domestic and international illegality for more than fifteen years after 9/11; Trump's fascism is simply the next, perhaps last, stage of that process.

I started having the thought of total disengagement in the early years of the Obama administration, and it is only now that I'm articulating it, but I think I was on the right track even then. What if, instead of eight years of Obama-era activism, the people had delegitmized politics by not voting, not participating, not commenting, simply retreating into private life? And by that I mean constructing healthy, nonconsumerist, creative lives, carved with difficulty out of the disastrous environment capitalism forces us to live in, but otherwise oblivious to it? Is that not all the more necessary now that neoliberal capitalism, from everything I understand of it, is in a mortal fight to the end with the health of the planet and all living species, a fight that for a while now I have believed cannot last beyond the middle of this century?

We empowered Trump by empowering Obama, focusing, unfortunately, on the politics of personality, since our liberal intelligentsia is the least equipped of any comparable entity in modern history to articulate matters at a coherent conceptual or theoretical level. We empowered Obama's war against Muslim nations and against Muslim and Latino immigrants at home, by asking for small mercies, by being pleased with legalistic cover for what are ultimately irredeemable illegalities. How will the next Democratic president, an Andrew Cuomo or Kirsten Gillibrand, be any different? The point is to end empire, the point is to want to accelerate its end, which Trump surely is embarked on doing already.

Let me go back to some historical parallels, particularly from my study of fascist Italy. The conservative (corporate) establishment of that time chose Mussolini's law and order message over the turbulence Italy's socialist parties had heralded during the Biennio Rosso (1919-1920), the two years of red uprising after the end of World War I. Had the communists and socialists been able to get along, there would have been no fascism. In our case, we don't have communist or socialist parties, just variants of slightly more progressive thinking than the reigning neoliberalism, but even these sides cannot get along, because, for one thing, identity politics fatally compromises class consciousness of any kind. There is no viable political party to represent the interests of the people!

Mussolini faced resistance from socialists, such as Antonio Gramsci and others whom he imprisoned, in the first three years of his reign, before he consolidated his dictatorship and ended all pretense of democratic institutions in 1925. I have to say that the amount of resistance we've already seen in response to Trump, from the judiciary to inside the intelligence bureaucracies to ordinary people who have come out in historic numbers to try to protect the rights of their fellow citizens who happen to be from other countries, is surprising and welcome, and unlike anything we saw in the Bush years. I see this situation as comparable to that between 1922-1925 in Italy, before Mussolini, in the crisis that ensued after the murder of the leading opposition socialist, Giacomo Matteoti, silenced the press and any political opposition once and for all.

Does that mean that there will be a declaration of emergency, following which the press will be silenced? No, again because we are the world's dominant power, and the ideology (neoliberalism) that has spawned fascism was already prevalent in the media, the academy, and all the institutions of civil society, so there need not be that level of disruption.

I would ask the question, what enormity can one think of that would bring American society to a halt? Mass deportations? They're already happening, but what if they escalate to a target of ten to twenty million people? I don't think we have the power to resist. Of course the escalation of multiple wars in the Middle East is inevitable and would just be a continuation of Clinton-Bush-Obama policies, but what about the deployment of tactical nuclear weapons against, say, Iran? Would that be the turning point that brings society to a halt, and renews democracy?

I have thought for a long time that there is *no* bridge too far to cross, no enormity so great that it would end our ideas of American exceptionalism, an innocence that the resisters are feeding into, strengthening it all the time, even as the noose tightens around our necks.

But what does it mean to disengage? People have children to feed, jobs to perform, which in many cases may be jobs that help people, in education and social services for example. But there are also single people, younger people, those with greater mobility and options. If one can leave the country, I would say, do so; America is not a project worth salvaging. A fascist power that is the leading roadblock to world progress, in places as far away as South America and India, is not something to devote one's only precious life to. Even if Hitler is winning, do you want to join him as an ally, do you want to entertain ideas of moderating and refining and containing him, do you want to keep looking for the good Germans to overturn the oppressive order once and for all? And what if, in that effort, you become collateral damage?

Instead of the wasted energy spent during the Obama years to try to normalize what is ultimately not normalizable, i.e. the unconstitutional regime that has existed since 9/11, what if young people had refrained from investing hope in politics? All kinds of ethical choices outside capitalism then become possible, ranging from living communally on a small scale, reclaiming territory outside the stressful purview of urban gentrification, growing one's own food and exiting the capitalist health care system, and engaging in barter and cooperation to create a sustainable and aesthetically fulfilling existence. Call it socialism, call it anarchism, but to want to want to reform the unreformable only empowers those who want to take away the very possibility of alternative spaces.

If I were a little younger, I would leave America and put down roots somewhere else; if there is a country where there seems a greater hope for promoting democracy, then that is a choice people should explore. Is America so much better than every place else? Why can't we take our democratic ideas elsewhere and make those places, not at the center of the fascist hegemony, better, by our example and productivity? Why should we feed this particular machine with our minds and bodies?

What needs to happen is to strengthen countries like Canada and those in Europe that are still struggling against fascism, and everywhere else there is hope in Latin America and Africa and Asia, against the global hegemony America wants to impose. If one is older or is restricted or does not have the mobility I speak of, then one can stay in place, but at the very least one should downshift, retreat from capitalism, and morally disengage from anything having to do with saving this country's place in world politics (i.e., empire). One can, out of a sense of duty, provide for one's children and family, but not be morally committed to the idea of America, which has become toxic beyond rescue, because it is not America of the old we're talking about, but a new form of neoliberal fascism that is in mortal combat with the principle of life itself.

The preservation of life is all-important, not the principle of America, and let me say that I am sure that these two principles are in absolute conflict at the moment. Moral disengagement is a form of civil resistance, perhaps the most powerful form.

The main counterargument to what I'm saying would be, Are we just going to let the fascists take over? Will we let them do whatever they want to do, deport ten million people, start catastrophic wars? Well, aren't we already? That moment was long ago, when we could have chosen social democracy over neoliberalism, but we as a people, particularly our intelligentsia, decided not to, over a period of thirty years; more specifically, we deliberately sacrificed whatever remained of our democracy to make sure that the collective good had no chance of ascendancy, when we went for Hillary over Bernie.

Suppose all public resistance, i.e. engagement, ceases tomorrow. What would happen? Would Trump be more or less emboldened to expel ten million people or start an unprecedented war in the Middle East? He's going to do it regardless, but his power in doing so will be much greater, it will again come packaged as a real war of ideas, when he does so, if resistance in the way we think of it continues. In the absence of reaction, his actions will go forward anyway but will not have the same meaning. Mass deportation has been going on for twenty years, the wars in the Middle East in their current form have been going on for twenty-five years, and they will continue to happen, but our participation gives more strength to these violations, gives them legitimacy because there is an appearance of a democratic contest.

If we have to boycott someone, shouldn't we start with the Democratic party? Can resistance operate through a vehicle so compromised? Shouldn't we delegitimize it by nonparticipation?

I am arguing that the only moral thing to do in reaction to the fascist onset is to disengage, in every way possible: physically, economically, spiritually, philosophically. And I am arguing that to engage in any way is to be morally supportive of fascism—which probably includes this screed as well, and any thought processes I might have toward fascism, because in that way too I am strengthening it. I only know that the normal democratic means are no longer relevant, since we have nobody in power to represent our moral position, and nor are we likely to, now that things have gone this far.

Mussolini experienced the peak of his power long after the consolidation of his dictatorship in the 1925-1929 period; it was in the 1930s, all the way up to the Ethiopian war in 1936, that consensus was greatest toward the fascist principle. It took abject defeat in World War II to finally end fascism, and for people to come out of the woodwork and claim that they had always been antifascist, even if they hadn't expressed it so. Hitlerism likewise only ended with total defeat in war. Every totalitarianism, once it gets going past a certain point, ends in the same familiar way, there is simply no historical precedent for a peaceful conclusion. I need not spell out in any more detail what awaits American fascism, and what people have to think about doing for their own safety and well-being, to protect the only life they have been given and that is now under dangerous assault by the determined enemies of life itself.

Are Trump and Mussolini Cut from the Same Cloth? Eleven Key Lessons from Historical Fascism

"Fascism is a religion. The twentieth century will be known in history as the century of fascism." — Benito Mussolini

I'd like to draw some comparisons and contrasts between our present situation and that of fascist Italy between 1922-1945. I choose fascist Italy rather than Nazi Germany because it has always seemed to me a better comparison. Nazi Germany was the extreme militarist, racist, and totalitarian variant of Italian fascism, which was more adaptable, pragmatic, rooted in reality, and also more incompetent, ineffectual, and half-hearted, all of which seem true to our condition today. Italy was the original form, while Germany was an offshoot, and although there have been many European and some Latin American varieties of fascism since then, the Italian model was the first and the one that has had the most lasting influence.

Mussolini drew on strong existing European currents such as anarchosyndicalism, wanting to offer the world an alternative to what he saw as the failures of the Western democracies. His was a revolutionary agenda, designed to turn the world order upside down, rooted deeply in romantic and even avant-garde sensibilities. To see fascism as stemming ultimately from liberalism might sound surprising, but this is true of both socialism as well as fascism, because finally it is liberalism's principle of human perfectibility from which these impulses derive. Fascism, we might say, is liberal romanticism gone haywire. In its healthy state, liberalism gives us constitutional democracy, but in its unhealthy state we end up with totalitarianism.

Futurism, one of the leading modernist movements of the time, fed easily into fascism. F. T. Marinetti, who believed in war as "hygiene," was a keen Mussolini supporter, as was the playwright Luigi Pirandello, though he had a different aesthetic tendency. Many philosophers, academics, and artists were already sick of the mundane, transactional, enervating nature of democracy under leaders like Giovanni Giolitti, prime minister several times in the two decades preceding fascism.

Benedetto Croce, on the other hand, was the great Italian idealist philosopher, an optimistic Hegelian who believed that liberal constitutionalism was forever on the move, boosted by the Italian Risorgimento (unification) of the mid-nineteenth-century, even if its progress couldn't always be detected. Mussolini never openly persecuted Croce, partly for reasons of credibility—some internal criticism had to be allowed to preserve the façade of diversity of opinion—but mostly because, with a slight twist, Croce's Hegelian logic can easily lead to fascism.

To discuss Italian fascism in the context of Trumpism is not to draw silly one-on-one comparisons, because many material factors are different today, but to understand current developments there must be some historical basis for analysis. What this exercise attempts is to show that the myth of American exceptionalism is just that, a myth, and that we have traveled so far from our national founding impulses that other tendencies, namely forms of what used to be considered peculiarly European anxieties, have now become the defining features of our polity.

1. Fascism rechannels economic anxiety.

The German condition in the 1920s, with the economic instability then prevalent, is well-known, but this was also true of European countries in general in the wake of World War I. Especially after the Russian Revolution, the urgent question for all of Europe became: was socialism the right path, or capitalism? And in either case, was a new political order required?

In Italy, socialism became quite popular after the war, making industrialists and large agriculturalists very worried. The fascist squads, which at first had arisen spontaneously, came in handy to break the back of socialist cooperatives, both in industry and agriculture, particularly in northern Italy which was more advanced than the south. In the early part of his career, the opportunist Mussolini was anti-war (he didn't want Italy to join the First World War), as were socialists in general, but during the course of World War I he changed his tune. Evidence shows that he was financed by oligarchic foreign interests who wanted Italy to get into the war, which of course it did.

For the same money men, the question became, after the war, what to do with the mobilized energy of the arditi, or the squadrists? The original fascists, Mussolini included, were very socialist in inclination, and their manifestos reflected that. Mussolini's initial program for fascism could pass, with some changes, as an egalitarian dream. The founders of fascism were big on workers' rights, expropriation of leading industries, and even women's right to equality. The violent contest between socialists and fascists in the countryside had already abated by the time Mussolini came to power. Yet the oligarchic powers sought, in Mussolini, a figure to permanently channel and mobilize the violent social energy on behalf of capitalism.

The most recent phase of globalization, which took off during the 1990s, has created similar anxieties around the world as the class dislocations following World War I. For the elites who propagated the Washington Consensus in the 1990s, supported by such popularizers as Thomas Friedman, there was nothing complicated about globalization: incomes would rise around the world, inequality would fall and liberal tolerance would flourish. This rosy picture is so far from reality as to be laughable, and it is a truth evident to the world's peoples, except for the transnational elites still beholden to the abstract propositions. Thus the question arises again, with as much urgency as in the aftermath of the Russian Revolution: what shall be the world's economic order? Is it possible to conceive, at this late date, of globalization with a human face? Or is something more revolutionary needed?

The problem today is that socialism, unfortunately, got discredited in the eyes of liberals in the West because of the failed Soviet experiment. Socialism did not have to go the authoritarian route, but that is sadly how it turned out. So today we have a clear problem, i.e., burgeoning inequality on an almost unprecedented scale, and no ideological solution in sight, at least not one that majorities of liberals can agree on.

Into this vacuum, fascists all over the Western world are entering to redirect the majority white population's nervousness into xenophobic and imperialist aims. Each country, depending on its power structure, will pursue these aims, once it succumbs to the fascist virus, differently. It is worth remembering, however, that it was liberalism, with its absurd triumphant mentality in the wake of the collapse of the Soviet Union, that took away movement toward any form of socialism as a legitimate path, and therefore made the rise of fascism inevitable.

2. Liberal institutions have already been fatally weakened.

We are currently lamenting Trump's evisceration of the media and other institutions of democracy, but he would not be having such success, at least with one half of the population, if those institutions were not already seriously compromised. It is easy to dismiss his mockery of the "fake media," but before Trump did anyone take the media, with some venerable exceptions, seriously anyway? The mass media have never been interested in the nuances of policy, and are focused instead on personality, celebrity, and spectacle. Most of the print media are also compromised because of loyalty to American exceptionalism.

It is no coincidence that Trump has merged his critique of the "fake media" with exceptionalism, because it allows him to present the media as tools of a discredited ideology. Before Trump, the media were tied, as a general rule, to the consensus on neoliberalism, and their bias became all the more evident during the last campaign. When it comes to telling the truth about power, the media have not been interested in doing so for a long time. They may now be reacting viscerally against Trump, because of the crude way in which he takes on their shallowness, but it doesn't mean anything to his supporters. Trump's critique of the media applies to all our liberal institutions prior to his arrival on the scene.

Mussolini's fascist program landed in the middle of deep disillusionment with liberal institutions. Italy had experienced a rapid spurt of growth due to industrialization in the late nineteenth and early twentieth centuries, but the rewards weren't equally distributed. The south was poor and undeveloped, overcome by feudal values, while the north was unsure about empowering labor to share the fruits of growth. The strong labor movement started shading into anarcho-syndicalism, quite similar to the original fascist manifesto. The situation is not exactly comparable today, because ours is a mature economy with declining traditional industrial sectors, while Italy's was an emerging economy with growing industries, but the sense that the institutions of democracy were failing to support a fair standard of living was widespread.

The Italian parliamentary system was marked by a tendency toward "transformismo" (transformism), to which our strongest parallel would be Bill (or Hillary) Clinton's triangulation (in many ways Clinton can be seen as a parallel to Giolitti, with the same ability to throw doubt on the health of liberal democracy, even as deals are cut right and left). Transformismo, or triangulation, appeals to career civil servants, politicians, and media people, but its chameleon-like tendency to absorb the ideas of the opposition and to neutralize them and make them invisible leaves a profoundly disillusioning aftertaste. Ideology desperately wants to make a comeback, which was true in transactional Italy, and is certainly true of America now.

3. Internal strongmen tussles don't mean anything.

In the beginning Mussolini didn't seem the most obvious choice to lead the fascist movement. Italy's best-known provocateur, Gabriele d'Annunzio, a flamboyant writer with a continental reputation, beat him to it by organizing a militia to lay siege to Fiume, a small territory on the northeast coast, part of the unredeemed lands claimed by the irredentist movement. In his short-lived siege, d'Annunzio perfected a fascist style—harangues prompting back-and-forth exchanges from balconies overlooking vast public squares, the symbolic elaboration of the myth of martyrdom in the cause of the nation, and the articulation of an emotional method for communicating reality—that Mussolini, and all later fascists, would adopt. D'Annunzio—a legendary womanizer and decadent—was one of the most colorful of all Europeans, and his peculiar interpretation of Nietzschean values has become a permanent challenge to liberal democracy.

But when push came to shove, Mussolini was seen as the more pliable agent of fascist change by his corporate benefactors, and Mussolini was quick to sideline d'Annunzio's claim to leadership. There were always more assertive fascists around than Mussolini—for example, Roberto Farinacci, the *ras* (or leader) of Cremona, who later became fond of Hitler's henchmen—but Mussolini was able to keep them in check. He was a master at playing one competitor against another, exploiting their vulnerabilities to always stay in power. The squadrist militias under control of the provincial *ras*, like Farinacci and others, were at first used by Mussolini to send terror into the hearts of wavering capitalists, and later, in different stages, were controlled and even neutralized as competing power centers, all of them absorbed in the mostly subservient National Fascist Party (PNF).

At the moment, Trump is our Farinacci, the most assertive of the *ras*, compared to whom all the cabinet secretaries—even the ones who most frighten us for their racism (attorney general Jeff Sessions) or Islamophobia (DHS secretary John Kelly)—seem tame in comparison.

No matter the insanity of the secretaries in charge of the environment, education, energy, or other departments, none seems as willing to openly flaunt the rule of law as Trump. Or we can say that in our case the showman d'Annunzio has taken power, rather than a more grounded journalist-tuned-politician like Mussolini. We confront the speculative exercise of trying to imagine how it would have turned out for fascism had d'Annunzio, not Mussolini, been the leader.

Nonetheless, we ought not to be swayed by the temporary ascendancies of this or that group within the fascist hierarchy, whether it is Steve Bannon or Michael Flynn who rises or falls, because fascism is greater than the individuals who make up its core at any given moment. Fascism does require the strongman at the center to make it move, yet if a given personality fails to do the job another can be found as replacement.

4. Fascism keeps mutating.

Before fascism was formalized by Mussolini in 1919, organizing the scattered energies of the displaced combatants, it was in many ways an aesthetic movement. It was certainly radically socialist in orientation, with a strong attraction to equality for workers. Then, just before taking power, it became a movement for capitalist law and order, suppressing the demands of socialists. Once in power it adopted some of the modes of parliamentary behavior, but with great irritation, as it sought to preserve a democratic façade. After the consolidation of the dictatorship in 1925, it became almost a developmental state, strongly interested in Italy's economic growth. A corporatist state, with strong autarkic goals (such as the "Battle for Wheat," to make Italy self-sufficient, or the reclamation of the Pontine Marshes), was clearly articulated, eliciting approval from the world's leading capitalist powers.

With the onset of worldwide depression, however, fascism realized the intractability of economic problems and turned its attention to imperialism. The PNF, which had become relatively quiet during the period of capitalist development, was revived as a harsh ideological force, with growing tentacles in every part of Italian society. This phase began in the early 1930s and lasted until defeat in World War II. Fascism was not particularly racist to begin with, as Mussolini, like most Italians, took exception to Nazi anti-Semitism; but as Italy threw in its lot with Germany in the late 1930s, "scientific" racism became a central fascist platform. After Mussolini was overthrown by his own Grand Council in 1943, for the last two years of the war he held fort in the Republic of Salò, in the northern part of Italy, supported by Hitler's fading power. The Republic of Salò backtracked to the original socialist principles enunciated at the formation of fascism.

What this shows is that fascism is highly adaptable to different needs and conditions, just as its opposite, democracy, is similarly flexible. This also suggests that fascism is a viable ideology just like democracy, because it can appear in different guises at different times, even under the same leadership, without losing credibility. In considering Trump and the movement he has sparked, we would be better off looking at the overall aims of the regime, rather than get carried away by feints in one direction or another. Their aim, it should be clear, is to end democracy, since that is the energy fascism feeds on.

Trump is fully capable of showing an apparently "presidential" side, for example in his first speech to congress. The priority has shifted from eradicating immigrants to passing the neoliberal agenda on taxation, social spending, education, energy, and the environment, so a slightly modified relationship is needed with the corporate world and the media for the immediate future, which Trump should easily be able to accomplish. Mussolini, though an inveterate atheist, made peace with the Vatican, in the famous Lateran Accords of 1929, abandoning his most cherished beliefs in order to gain the complicity of the Catholic church. Earlier in the 1920s, he installed corporate-friendly ministers to work with Italy's industrialists to enact an agenda they could be comfortable with. Such mutations are par for the course for fascists, they're nothing to get excited about.

5. Fascism is eternally recurring.

Just as democracy is eternal, so is fascism. There were always authoritarian or dictatorial responses to democracy since the beginning of modern civilization, but fascism, with its imprint of spectacle, theater, and mass communication, was a particular permutation that arose once the Western democracies had been consolidated. Italy and Germany were two of the late bloomers, but democracy had mostly been attained by the time they turned to fascism. Fascism could not have arisen were democracy still an evolving condition, as was true of parts of the West in the nineteenth century. So fascism is an indication of maturity, once democracy's initial bloom is off.

Many historians were eager to write off Italy's fascist experience as an aberration, as something so abnormal that it did not properly belong to Italian culture, but the opposite is true. Fascism will often borrow the symbolism, legal architecture, and academic norms of preexisting society, rather than throw them overboard. In Italy's case, all of the existing tendencies of aesthetic modernism came in handy, as well as the legacies of socialist, anarchist, and syndicalist cultures. In northern cities like Turin and Milan, fascism flourished side by side with avant-garde political and cultural thinking. Once the dominant liberal culture succumbed, it wasn't as difficult to impose fascism's content upon the less democratic south's institutions.

Fascism was not an aberration for Italy, nor is this the case anywhere it occurs. It is inherent in the DNA of any given culture, an authoritarian side that goes along with, and is even a necessary prop for, democracy. The interwar years marked industrialization's maturity in the Western world, which had been preceded by a huge burst of globalization, leading up to World War I. A fascism drawing energy from the masses employed in industrialized occupations, as was the case between the wars, is going to manifest very differently than the post-industrial environment of twenty-first-century America. But the differences are more stylistic than foundational.

6. Of course it's a minority affair.

To note that Trump did not win the popular vote (as was true of Bush in 2000), does not take away from the power of fascism. Given civilized norms in a democratic society, it is always going to be difficult for fascists to muster an outright numerical majority. The point is their relative strength in terms of raw power. Moreover, in periods of emergencies (such as Bush after 9/11 and in the lead-up to the Iraq war), more than a majority can usually be cobbled. This speaks strongly to the hidden patriotic foundation of what passes as liberalism, its inherent weakness which can so easily be converted to mass militarism.

Mussolini, though he established his regime on the myth of the March on Rome, was actually appointed by King Victor Emmanuel III when Mussolini seemed like the only figure, compared to the discredited liberal politicians, who could bring order to the country. Trump too is trying to make predictions of chaos and violence a self-fulfilling prophecy, but this is a staple of all fascist regimes: they bring about and thrive on the disorder that they then claim to be the only ones to be able to suppress. There was actually no such thing as the March on Rome, the King had already invited Mussolini to Rome to come and form the government, when the march took place. Had the King given the order—and this looked possible until the last fateful moment—the army would have easily crushed the ragtag bunch of nobodies who had showed up from all parts of Italy.

Only a small minority need give overt consent. The rest can be quiet, or complacent, or complicit, unless they feel their personal security threatened, for example because of war that might spin out of control. That is all that's needed for fascism to go on its merry way, so it's quite beside the point to argue its minority status. Most bloody revolutions are minority affairs.

7. There is an ideology behind the chaos of ideologies.

Just as Italian historians after the fact claimed that fascism was an aberration that didn't belong to Italy's history proper, contemporary observers often insisted that there was never a fascist ideology. Partly this is because of the mutational aspect of fascism. But primarily this is due to intellectual laziness. Liberal scholars, after all, are not likely to credit their mortal opponent with ideological clarity. We too, lazily, ascribe the same lack of ideology to Trumpism, and interpret events in terms of personality and contingency. I would say that fascist ideology has always, since its inception a hundred years ago, been so strong that it takes democracy an extremely favorable environment, and a huge amount of luck, to sustain itself.

Fascist ideology aims for nothing but to weaken and end democracy. It is democracy's successes, whether in Weimer Germany, or in a strange way in Giolitti's Italy, or in countercultural America of the 1960s, that breed the opposite tendency which wants to swallow it up.

Mussolini pursued imperialistic goals in wanting an empire in North Africa, East Africa, and the Balkans, but was his pursuit of empire (the New Rome) the same as Britain's, for example, in the nineteenth century? For Britain, the empire made financial sense. For Italy, all its wars were financially ruinous (and this has been true of our own wars after 9/11 as well), exerting unsustainable pressures. But to the extent that the wars undermined democracy, breeding fascism at home, they were certainly successful. In our present and future wars, that is the criterion we must keep in mind. It's not what a particular policy is doing to the budget or our diplomatic standing or the state of the culture, but how a policy undermines democracy.

8. Its cultural style makes no sense to elites.

This is where I felt the Bush incarnation of fascism fell short, and this is where Trump too is having a difficult time. Milo Yiannopoulos proved in the end to be too exotic even to his sponsors at Breitbart, and the campy, decadent, d'Annunzian style, of which Milo is an heir, has its limits in evangelical America, committed to bourgeois verities despite the fascistic overlay. Our homegrown brew of Fox News, Breitbart, Alex Jones, border militias like the Minutemen, millenarian Christianity, the Tea Party, and gun culture, combined with simplistic beliefs in "free market" capitalism and American exceptionalism, seems to me a particularly tame cultural concoction. It doesn't have traction with anyone with the least amount of liberal education. Mussolini was working with more resonant cultural stuff, as the emergence of industrial capitalism since the Risorgimento had set up a cultural platform that was malleable enough to work for fascism.

Trump and his successors will have to work with less potent stuff. So-called "conspiratorial" thinking is a unifying strand—I already mentioned Alex Jones—which connects many of the strands of ultra-conservative thinking throughout the past century. The reds are Jews are Muslims, the substitutions are not that difficult to make. But although the elites will remain incredulous toward fascism's cultural style, there seems to be enough of a momentum, with all the tendencies beginning to attain critical mass together. Thus the successful transition from Bush to Trump, which suggests that our homegrown fascist style is strong enough now not to need a leader.

Masculinity—or shall we say faux masculinity—is an important part of this cultural style, perhaps the reason why Milo couldn't last. It is a reaction to the perceived effeminacy of liberalism, and is a blast, along with racism, against what is seen as the failed order. Fascism relies on activation of our most atavistic, violent, and primitive selves, by wanting to return women to invisibility, along with condemning the darker races. Needless to say, Italian fascism reconstructed women as facilitators of warrior-masculinity in all the active fields of life, depriving women of organizational visibility even when they were outstanding fascists.

9. Fascism leads inexorably to suicidal war.

It's possible to argue that Mussolini was sucked into World War II against his will, because he knew it was going to end his regime since Italy was not prepared. We might credit it to Hitler's powers of manipulation over Mussolini that Italy entered a disastrous war. The truth is that from the beginning Mussolini had been biding his time to exert Italian power abroad. He had no respect for diplomats, exactly like Trump, and chose to go his own way, believing himself to be a master strategist. He made increasingly assertive forays into warmaking, from the little adventure in Corfu in 1923, all the way to the massive commitment to the Ethiopian war in 1936, along the way proclaiming himself "protector of Islam."

Fascism, like all forms of government which are not based on the consent of the majority, requires more and more energy to keep the population under control as time goes by. Once the façade of virile domesticity starts getting exposed, war becomes the only option to keep the regime going. Fascism always claims that war is not of its choosing, that it is forced into war by others, but it is a voluntary, even eager, action to perpetuate the regime. At some point, the boomeranging negative energy—violence inflicted upon the fascist power in return—is so great that the tide of opinion turns. Even if war might be fought to an end, the internal consensus, including amongst fascist believers, is gone. We are, obviously, a long way from that.

10. Racism is inherent to fascism.

It is absolutely key that Trump began his campaign by proclaiming a genocidal manifesto against Mexicans—and then Muslims and Arabs—and has continued to keep it as his central point of action. Because fascism is not competing on an even ideological terrain—most people in any civilized country are not given to violence—it must imagine enemies powerful enough to sustain a majority reaction.

Mussolini and his lieutenants used to mock Hitler's racial animus, both before and after he became chancellor, holding that Italians had no anti-Semitic sentiment, which was quite true. Some of Mussolini's most ardent early supporters were Jewish, and he had prominent Jewish lovers, like his biographer Margherita Sarfatti. But after the goodwill from the Ethiopian war started fading in the late 1930s, and a closer alliance with Germany became inevitable, Italy turned around and instituted an official anti-Semitism that deprived Jews of their honor, property, and basic rights. The situation never got as bad as in Germany, with most Italians harboring deep suspicions toward the newfound anti-Semitism and the construction of Italians as a superior Aryan race, but the damage was done.

Just as war is inevitable, so is virulent racism, both go together in fascism. One provides an external enemy, while the other provides an internal enemy. If they can be linked together—the worldwide Jewish banking conspiracy, or the worldwide Islamic terror conspiracy—then all the better. War becomes more comprehensible, for fascist supporters, when the internal enemy is attached to the endless cycle of wars abroad, said to stem from the same root threat to virile nationalist probity.

11. No form of resistance works.

And finally, how do you fight fascism? Is there a magic formula, has anything ever worked, or are we, too, assuming that we are launched on our own fascist cycle, doomed to repeat the familiar pattern until the end? Can liberalism awaken itself in time, once it recognizes the mortal danger, to defeat fascism? Will the citizenry in a liberal democratic nation, once prompted to the threat, find resources it hadn't counted on before to invalidate and eventually suppress fascism? Can violence, in short, be defeated by nonviolence? We would have to presume this to be true, unless we accept that liberals would take up arms to defeat fascism, which is not likely and probably defeatist anyway.

The Italian press, when Mussolini took over the country, was extremely vigorous. Political parties of every persuasion were highly energized, and they all had their vocal newspapers. Mussolini himself had run socialist newspapers—first *Avanti!* and then *Il Popolo d'Italia*—for the majority of his adult career, and knew that to neutralize the press was his first order of business. He did so in stages, eventually ushering in a regime of complete censorship after 1925, particularly after failed assassination attempts gave him the excuse. He installed fascist stooges at all the newspapers and carefully monitored their every word for the rest of his regime. Loyalty oaths were likewise instituted everywhere, from higher education to civil service. The institutions appeared the same, they were not abolished, but they had been hollowed out.

The press went underground, numerous political activists went into exile, particularly in France, and the communists, socialists, conservatives, liberals, monarchists, and Catholics bid their time, engaging in resistance when they could, hoping for an awakening of mass consciousness. Neutralizing the church with the Lateran Accords, and thereafter depoliticizing Catholic Action, the organization competing with Mussolini's numerous social and leisure organizations, was important, and the church never regained its full voice. The exiles abroad were killed or hurt, and many died in the Spanish Civil War. It was not until Mussolini's own Grand Council deposed him in 1943, when it was clear that Italy had lost the war, that the country divided into two and the partisans emerged to slowly recover Italian democracy in stages.

The Italians tried every form of resistance we can imagine, including getting themselves and their families killed or imprisoned, as countless lives were lost in the fascist tyranny. Nothing worked. Nothing ever works until fascism's logic, the logic of empire, stands discredited to the point where no denial, no media cover-up, is possible anymore.

Some final thoughts.

The thing to notice is how fascism, in all the places it's been known to arise, converts an admittedly minority point of view into a mass energy that soon overwhelms every civilized instinct. Perhaps Trump doesn't need to do this footwork, perhaps much of this foundational work was already accomplished in the Bush era. What should really concern us is that fascism now seems to have a certain stability that we have not known from earlier models which relied on a single charismatic leader to operate. Despite the Obama interlude, Trump has resumed where Bush in his most feverish mood had left off. This suggests that fascism has become permanently stabilized in this country. It is the most worrisome aspect of the present situation.

Fascism would never have gotten such traction here had liberalism not already succumbed, over the course of forty years, to various abridgements of rights in the name of community or security or risk-aversion, which defines much of liberal discourse today. Fascism cannot thrive on true individualism, which is inherently opposed to mass delusions, but liberalism took the lead long ago in giving up individualism for forms of imagined community. This is ultimately the breeding ground for fascism, and this is why it is an affair that envelopes all of us, not just a certain segment of the population that we can condemn as fascist and be done with it.

One remarkable similarity—among many others—between Trump and Mussolini is their total preoccupation with coverage in the media. Trump regularly consumes the "shows," apparently getting most of his news and information from there, and has little use for time-consuming memoranda and policy documents. He monitors, obsessively, what the media says about him. Mussolini, it could be said, was almost a full-time journalist during his twenty-three years of power. Just as Trump's Oval Office desk is littered with the "papers," so was Mussolini's time taken up with controlling every word that was printed about the regime. Obsessively detailed "veline" went out every day to the country's newspapers, instructing them on how to interpret every event. There were to be no pictures of Mussolini appearing in less than heroic posture, no mention of crime or poverty or violence, no disparagement of the fascist regime.

The inordinate amount of time Mussolini—like Trump—spent cultivating image does not have anything to do with a personality disorder. It has to do with democracy's failure to live up to its egalitarian ideals, so that the lie about equality becomes more important than actual equality. The liberal democratic and fascist authoritarian versions of this lie have much in common. It is futile to look for tanks on the street as a marker of fascism; there were no tanks in the streets in fascist Italy either. What is important to notice are the weak spots of liberal democracy, which fascism exploits, such as the gradual loss of faith in our voting and electoral systems. What is important to notice is the symbolic order which becomes more and more different until one day it becomes a vehicle for a different ideology than the majority ever bargained for.

About the Author

Anis Shivani is a fiction writer, poet, literary critic, and political analyst living in Houston, Texas. His critically acclaimed books include *Anatolia and Other Stories*, *The Fifth Lash and Other Stories*, *Karachi Raj: A Novel*, *My Tranquil War and Other Poems*, *Whatever Speaks on Behalf of Hashish: Poems*, *Soraya: Sonnets*, *Against the Workshop: Provocations, Polemics, Controversies*, and *Literary Writing in the Twenty-First Century: Conversations*. His work appears widely in such journals as the *Yale Review*, *Georgia Review*, *Southwest Review*, *Boston Review*, *Threepenny Review*, *Michigan Quarterly Review*, *Antioch Review*, *Black Warrior Review*, *Western Humanities Review*, *Boulevard*, *Pleiades*, *AGNI*, *Fence*, *Denver Quarterly*, *Volt*, *Subtropics*, *New Letters*, *Times Literary Supplement*, *London Magazine*, *Cambridge Quarterly*, *Contemporary Review*, *Meanjin*, *Fiddlehead*, *Dalhousie Review*, *Antigonish Review*, and elsewhere. He has also written for many magazines and newspapers including *Salon*, *Daily Beast*, *AlterNet*, *CommonDreams*, *Counterpunch*, *Truthout*, *Huffington Post*, *Texas Observer*, *In These Times*, *Boston Globe*, *San Francisco Chronicle*, *Kansas City Star*, *Pittsburgh Post-Gazette*, *Baltimore Sun*, *Charlotte Observer*, *Austin American-Statesman*, and elsewhere. He is the winner of a Pushcart Prize, and a graduate of Harvard College.

Most political analysts were taken by surprise by Donald Trump's success during the campaign and even more so by his eventual win. The author of this book consistently predicted victory for Trump over Hillary Clinton, should the Democratic party fail to nominate Bernie Sanders, which is precisely what happened. Removing the analysis from matters of personality and contingency, this book seeks to identify the larger institutional and economic changes that have resulted in a rank political outsider such as Trump taking complete power in Washington and sidelining the liberal opposition in every branch of government. Is Trump a fascist, an authoritarian populist, a right-wing extremist, or someone who fits into an established pattern of American conservatism? Was identity politics the biggest loser in the election? What is the future of the Democratic party's appeal to and patronage by the financial class, and what happens when the other party is able to shear off, by demagogic appeals, a large part of the coalition that needs to hold if the meritocratic/neoliberal vision of the financial class is to achieve electoral success? Is there any chance that the Democratic party will undertake philosophical reform and go back to its original base from before the neoliberal ascendancy? Does neoliberalism explain everything that happened in this election, or are there residual factors outside this explanatory framework? How did the press, and the establishment in general, get it so wrong on so many counts throughout the last two years of buildup to this election, and what chance is there for accountability and course correction according to the facts on the ground? What is the Trump coalition? What is Trumpism? What should we expect from this movement, and what should we not? These and other crucial questions have assumed life-and-death importance for the body politic, especially for embattled minority groups feeling betrayed and abandoned by establishment politicians and intellectuals who failed to see the truth of what was going on in the country. These questions are addressed with stimulating clarity and vision in this book of essays that unfolds in real time along with the surge of populism on both left and right in the historic election campaign. The next chapter in American politics is only beginning. This book provides a sound intellectual platform from which to interpret and anticipate the direction of events in the age of Trump.

Made in the USA
Middletown, DE
16 August 2017